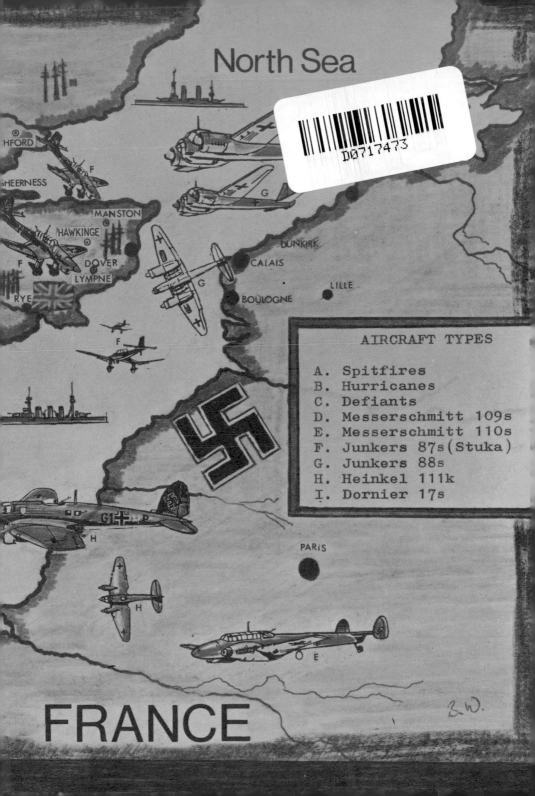

North Sea

AIRCRAFT TYPES

A. Spitfires
B. Hurricanes
C. Defiants
D. Messerschmitt 109s
E. Messerschmitt 110s
F. Junkers 87s (Stuka)
G. Junkers 88s
H. Heinkel 111k
I. Dornier 17s

FRANCE

EX LIBRIS

E.R.UREN.

EIGHTY FOUR DAYS

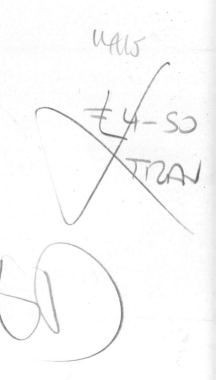

By the same Author:

BEYOND THE TUMULT
THE FIRESIDE V.C.

EIGHTY FOUR DAYS

BARRY WINCHESTER

A Rhyming Appreciation and Comment
on
THE BATTLE OF BRITAIN

With a Foreword by

Air Chief Marshal Sir Keith Park
GCB,KCB,CB,KBE,MC,DSC,DCL,MA.

THE SELMA PRESS
sussex

First published in Great Britain
by The Selma Press, 12 Boxes Lane, Horsted Keynes,
Sussex

© 1974 by Barry Winchester

ISBN 0 904272 00 1

Printed in Great Britain by
Charles Clarke (Haywards Heath) Ltd.
Haywards Heath, Sussex

To
Squadron Leader Geoffrey Wellum, DFC,
Spitfire pilot and living epitome of all
this rhyming tribute seeks to record.

CONTENTS

EIGHTY FOUR DAYS

CONTENTS

CONTENTS

CONTENTS

APPENDICES*

1. THE BATTLE OF BRITAIN - Facsimile of the Ministry of Information Booklet issued on behalf of the Air Ministry and distributed nationwide in 1941.
2. Facsimile Anti-Invasion leaflets issued nationwide.

* The material in the Appendices is Crown copyright and is reproduced by kind permission of the Controller, Her Majesty's Stationery Office.

FOREWORD

Air Chief Marshal Sir Keith Park, GCB, KCB, CB, KBE, MC, DSC, DCL, MA.

No amount of praise could be too great for Dowding's contribution to victory in this most crucial Battle of Britain. He was the architect and builder of Royal Air Force, Fighter Command, in the years preceding the Second World War. This I vouch for, having been his Chief of Staff from 1938 to 1940.

Many books have been written about the Battle of Britain and most have failed to appeal to the general public, being too long or too technical. Other books have been too scrappy to paint a clear picture.

Barry Winchester avoids these mistakes and, by his new approach to the subject - i.e. a mixture of verse and prose, has written a most readable and entertaining book.

26th December 1972

INTRODUCTION

My tapestry of woven verse
Relates at length, or sometimes terse,
Of dogfight battles overhead,
Of those who lived and those now dead;
In lone defiance called to stand
And fight for England's pleasant land.
To "See it Through" at any price;
"Go to it!" paying sacrifice
In blasted street or blackened shell;
Hold Freedom's Gate against all hell.
From tortured earth and crater slime,
I've pottered humble bits of rhyme.

Thro' many hours nostalgic pen
Has scrawled these pages, written when,
A prompted glimpse, a song perchance,
Might earn from friends a gaze askance,
As far from them my thoughts would flit,
To conjure visions herein writ;
Of shattered streets and splintered homes,
Dim silhouettes my mind still roams
In far off times, in days long gone,
Still vibrant with the bomber's drone.
Translated at more recent time
In fragment verse or detailed rhyme.

INTRODUCTION

Here then my metred summary.
Some good, I hope, some bad, maybe.
But all have root in fact and past;
The siren's wail, the bomber's blast,
The Messerschmitt death-stabbing rattle;
Those tangle-vapour webs of Battle;
That bloody tapestry of war,
Embroidered by both rich and poor,
With precious threads of human life
Expended freely in the strife.
Each has its place for good or worse
In this my book of humble verse.

PREFACE

This collection is largely based on the personal experiences of a boy who was fifteen years of age during the Battle. He saw much of the daylight fighting from either the saddle of a grocer's delivery tricycle in the streets of North London or garden shelters at the rear of countless homes in the Enfield district.

The Messerschmitt 110 that crashed into the sewage farm at Ponders End is no myth. Along with the Junkers 86 mentioned in ONE OF THE FEW, the Dornier that crashed at Southbury Road and the Stuka that blew up at Epping, mentioned in ONE OF THE MANY, these incidents were eagerly visited by the writer on his beloved bike in accordance with the current teenage pastime of 1940. Only actual characters have been changed on occasions as the writer felt prudent in these attempts to portray most aspects of the momentous Battle he witnessed. He had no true grasp of its importance at the time. The same could be truthfully said of most of the adults around him.

By September 1940, Douglas Bader, Stanford Tuck, Sailor Malan and countless other pilots, had become household words to the populace at large. To those of us who were either schoolboys, or just out of school, they were idols to which no modern pop star could even begin to compare.

Bader in particular had already become a living legend world-wide, and in my little sphere he was the sole object of an intense hero-worship which the privilege of later contact cemented into strong admiration. For this reason no apology is made for the legendary spice with which DRAKE'S HURRICANE is liberally sprinkled.

OUR EARLY WARNING SYSTEM is in memory of
a lovable black and white cat named Micky who literally
performed as described. I am sure that many London
felines had the same capacity.

TUCK'S LUCK requires little comment from me -
the entire content is factual - apart from recording my
great admiration in addition to my already offered
best wishes.

Despite countless books having been written, and a
superb film made on the subject, the complete story of
the Battle of Britain has yet to be told in its entire
complexity. Perhaps somewhat naturally to the schoolboys of the day, Spitfire pilots were stars of the daily
shift and counterplay enacted over our young heads.
But retrospectively, I realise the importance of roles
played by many unsung heroes with whom I must have
rubbed shoulders on the ground whilst my gaze was
skywards.

Intense activity in bomb-shattered streets was a
commonplace sight in an everyday setting. Sweating
Rescue Men struggled to recover living and dead from
perilous mounds of debris, which hours earlier had been
dearly treasured homes; ARP men and women coolly
created order in a ghastly tangle of smoke and dust-pall
chaos; ambulance personnel - men and women - stood
patiently by to receive and succour the maimed and
injured; urgent shouts and sobbing; soft words of comfort
against a background noise of boots crunching in a sea
of broken glass, were often drowned by the powerful
wail of yet more air raid sirens as a fresh wave of the
Luftwaffe assault was heralded. The sirens would fade
and murmur until before long, the then familiar drone

of bombers would be heard.

The crash of bombs and the distant rattle of machine-guns would cause everybody to look upwards momentarily. Golden lace-like vapour-trails would weave a tangled pattern across a glorious blue sky as the life and death struggle overhead painted yet another backdrop of incredible beauty. Then the stricken high-pitched wail of a doomed bomber would give rise to hoarse cheers from grimy men labouring in the aftermath of a previous raid. This was the Battle in perhaps its rawish aspect. But wherever such drama was enacted, there would be the inevitable canteens and the selfless women of the Salvation Army and the Women's Voluntary Service supplying tea to sweating men and soup to distressed citizens. Other personnel comforted women and children while assisting in the rescue and sorting out of personal treasures from shattered homes. Often on site too, would be those now near-forgotten men of the Demolition Squads whose task was to make threatening structures safe whilst working in co-operation with their colleagues of the Rescue teams.

Last, but by no means least, I would give humble tribute to those of the less obvious organizations which were equally vital in role during the Battle.

As always the "London bobby" shouldered the demands made upon him. You would find him organizing passable routes from chaotic road blocks and patiently dealing with countless questions and anxious enquiries. His was often the all too unenviable task of being the bearer of tragic tidings to bereaved families. You would frequently find him at the end of a deserted roped-off street, almost literally sitting on an unexploded bomb or mine, and I am sure that his polite, "I'm afraid you can't go up here, sir!" disguised a wealth of calm apprehension as he kept his lonely and perilous vigil. Many retired men returned to the force for war service, and a host of "specials" swelled the ranks of the "Met" Police. All were a credit to its traditions, and other police forces carried out similar tasks with comparable gallantry.

Men of the London Fire Brigade and the Auxiliary Fire Service performed tasks which were self-evident. But they were to reach the pinnacle of devotion and sacrifice in the ensuing Blitz, and nobody could be more proud of them, then and now, than the boy privileged to wear their uniform as a part-time nuisance, many years prior to recording this tribute. Of course, we had our ladies too, who somehow did their duty with exemplary bravery whilst looking after us at the same time.

One normally had to visit distant fields or gain special admission to the tops of high buildings to see the men of the Royal Observer Corps at work. Their role was vital to the work of Fighter Command and the ARP services, and nothing I could say would add to the well-deserved praise already bestowed upon them.

My final comment appertains to a body of men whose cool bravery and quiet gallantry were beyond praise - the soldiers and sailors of the Bomb Disposal Units. As a kid I sat round several bomb-holes with them whilst sharing their tea and pretending to be as brave as they. Naturally, I was terrified that the metal monster in the hole would blow us all to smithereens, and the fact that these men had long since rendered the thing harmless did little to quell my terror. In our back garden - on a rockery! - there still perches the tail-fin trophy of a German 500 lb bomb, given to me by the Canadian Captain who had defused it. Surely this unknown hero was the bravest man I ever met.

Thus was the setting for my viewpoint of the Battle of Britain way back in those historic days of 1940. It is my sincere hope that many will see themselves recorded anonymously in memoirs now humbly offered to the reader.

I would like to thank the Royal Sovereign Group for their kind permission to reproduce throughout EIGHTY FOUR DAYS, the Letraset Action Transfers from the Instant Picture Book Series by Patterson Blick. Most of the illustrations are from BATTLE OF BRITAIN and THE DAM BUSTERS. The aircraft appearing on the cover, designed by the Author, were painted for the same series by Dennis Knight.

EIGHTY FOUR DAYS owes its unique CHAPLAIN'S EPILOGUE to the Reverend Canon W. D. O'Hanlon, MA, Church of England Chaplain at Biggin Hill during the Battle. SONNET TO A WINDSOCK and 1940 MARRIAGE were written by him at that time.

I am deeply indebted to Geoff Chamberlain for his role in this and other books as "sounding board" and technical editor. A BLENHEIM'S GUNNER relates an experience which had lasting impact on his mind and was subsequently written at his request.

To Patrick Murray, MBE, FSA (Scot.), Curator of

the Museum of Childhood, Edinburgh, I extend my gratitude for research into children's papers.

For inestimable hours and great patience spent on editing and preparing the final manuscript, my heart-felt thanks to Susan Wilson.

Lastly, not leastwise, to Michael Wilson and my wife Eileen, my thanks for many months of great forbearance.

Barry Winchester

London 1972

AUTHOR'S NOTE

Since the Battle, historians have disputed the date of its commencement. Many accept that it started on 1st July 1940. However, all agree that the Battle ended on 31st October. Essentially, as its title portrays, EIGHTY FOUR DAYS accepts the original starting date of 8th August, delineated by the official Battle of Britain pamphlet. This was issued by the Ministry of Information in 1941 and is reproduced in the Appendices.

HURRICANES and SPITFIRES were Fighter Command's main weapons in the Battle. But three other types were involved and deserve recognition, despite the fact that chronologically the bulk of the actions in which they fought took place prior to 8th August.

THE GLOSTER GLADIATOR - A single seat bi-plane fighter, armed with four Browning machine-guns, with a maximum speed of 260 miles per hour, flew many patrols during August 1940 having shot down a Heinkel 111 in June. This aircraft gave valiant service in Norway and is immortalized by the famous three: Faith, Hope and Charity, which defended Malta so gallantly.

THE BOULTON-PAUL DEFIANT - Much was expected of this ill-conceived turret fighter. Based on World War One concepts, fighting was left to the gunner, the pilot having no forward-firing guns. Defiants were operated during the Battle by Nos. 264 and 141 Squadrons. 264 Squadron achieved some measure of success with this type over Dunkirk which seemed to have heralded a false promise, for on 19th July, twelve Defiants of 141 Squadron moved forward from West Malling to Hawkinge after breakfast. At lunchtime they were ordered off from Hawkinge to patrol the Folkestone area. Engine trouble aborted the take-off of three of their number and nine Defiants soon found themselves engaged in murderous combat with Bf 109s of Goering's "Richthofen Geschwader". The Defiants were massacred. Four of their number were shot down and two crashed. Only one wounded pilot parachuted to safety and four gunners died in their turrets. Three Defiants landed back at Hawkinge: one so severely damaged that it was written off, and although the gunner of this aircraft had baled out, he was never found. Despite this debacle, the Defiants of 264 Squadron were sent off from Manston in the early afternoon of 24th August. Two were shot down in the battle which ensued after two had collided on the ground prior to take-off. The remnants of the Squadron took-off again late in the same afternoon and one fell victim to a Bf 109 near Hornchurch. Defiants were then withdrawn from daylight fighting to assume a night-fighter role.

THE BRISTOL BLENHEIM - A twin-engined fighter, largely used for reconnaissance and escort work. Proving vulnerable to the Messerschmitt 109s, the Blenheim suffered many casualties until, like the Defiant, it was withdrawn to serve as a night-fighter during the Blitz. Tragedy overtook this aircraft on 24th August, by virtue of its close resemblance to the Junkers 88. Blenheims of No. 235 (Fighter) Squadron were misidentified and attacked by Hurricanes. One fell in flames with its crew of three dead; one was so severely damaged it became a write-off and the third needed extensive repairs. Fortunately the two crews of the latter aircraft were unhurt.

*
*

FOR GOD, KING AND COUNTRY

GENTLEMEN - THE KING!

How much does Freedom owe to His Late Majesty?
King George the Sixth who bore each burdened day
With dignity distinguished from the travesty
Of rabble-rousing Fuhrer and Duce.
Defender of the Faith in word and deed
Who quietly reigned thro' days of dark despair,
And in his kingly wisdom oft decreed
That all his people kept a Day of Prayer.

Can any doubt God's Blessing of Our King?
Not one of us who witnessed mighty works!
The 'Few' could be compared with David's sling;
That Great Deliverance from grim Dunkerque's
Unsheltered beach of Stuka dive-bomb hell,
Thro' any eyes a miracle must be.
What calmed the Channel's constant angry swell
For river-boat flotillas plying free?

The King who dared in evil's darkest day
To grasp the Hand of Faith when hope seemed gone;
More safe, he said, than any charted way,
And trusting in the King of kings led on.
Thus he spoke and reigned thro' fateful years,
Until he stood in Freedom's Finest Hour
Acknowledging the Nation's frenzied cheers;
King George of England by God's Grace and Power.

"The gratitude of every home in our Island, in our Empire, and indeed throughout the world, except in the abodes of the guilty, goes out to the British airmen, who, undaunted by odds, unwearied in their constant challenge and mortal danger, are turning the tide of world war by their prowess and by their devotion. Never in the field of human conflict was so much owed by so many to so few. "

Sir Winston Churchill, 1940

"The Royal Air Force Benevolent Fund is part of the conscience of the British Nation. A Nation without a conscience is a Nation without a soul. A Nation without a soul is a Nation that cannot live. "

Sir Winston Churchill, 1951

"The time will come, when thou shalt lift thine eyes
To watch a long-drawn battle in the skies.
While aged peasants, too amazed for words,
Stare at the flying fleets of wondrous birds.
England, so long mistress of the sea,
Where winds and waves confess her sovereignty,
Her ancient triumphs yet on high shall bear
And reign the sovereign of the conquered air."

THOMAS GRAY

1737

THE REASON WHY

I fell in love with England when upon my
    Father's knee
I learned of great traditions and unequalled
    history.
Of Captain Henry Morgan and the feat of
    Billy Bligh,
Of Nelson, Drake and Jellicoe, whose wake
    the albatri
Rejoiced to shadow scavenging on high-
    endurance wings
Which then became the symbol of those
    sky encounterings
My Father's generation saw above the
    bloody Somme
When canvas once the power of ships gave
    flight to gun and bomb.
Thus Bishop, Ball and Robinson kept faith
    at awesome height
To smite new tyrants in the sun or cloaked
    by daunting night.
These passed the Grail of Freedom's Flame
    to men I know or knew,
Who held it dear above all cost - the pilots
    of the 'Few'.

THE REASON WHY

And so today we hold in trust an ember's
    dying spark
Which kindled once a fearsome blaze
    dispelling evil's dark.
But yet the password 'courage' holds the
    power of fanning flame
To all who prize our heritage and love
    Old England's name.
All heights and depths, earth, seas and
    skies are steeped in her traditions,
Shall puny intellectuals and faint-heart
    politicians
Gain mandate now to quench that spark
    which England gave her sons?
For every Englishman that lives is dead -
    if England shuns.

T H E   P R E S E N T

Eyesore skyscrapers sprout from the Luftwaffe's excavation sites as unwitting monuments to the 'Few'. And Piccadilly's Eros has been taken over and used as a shrine by the unwashed freaks of an uncaring generation.

———— * ————
*

HIGH SUMMER

I contemplate the blue September sky - a Boeing etching
    wispy feathered-trace;
With wailing jets it speeds its way miles-high - on course
    to some far-distant unknown place - and then is gone.
My eyes still rove the calm and empty sky and
    contemplate the one-time battle spaces
Where once I saw young pilots fight and die with summer
    sunlight shining in their faces - and glory shone.
No work-shy hippy shouted then for peace - no freak-out
    students thronged to demonstrate;
All had to fight for Freedom's precious lease or else
    succumb to living-death and hate - and had we done
The world today would be a different place - but not the
    empty dream of those afraid;
We all would bow before a 'master-race' and hippies then
    would scream they were betrayed - until the gun. . . . .

High over London battles filled the sky and millions
    watched Death's Reaper giving chase;
Cascading bombs claimed those who were to die and
    London was a scarred but better place - for she was true
To all who fought for her and never lacked for courage to
    stare danger in the face;
She owned no cowards scared to be attacked and hoping
    chants for peace might serve in place - pretending new
And futile dreams could change a world that has to fight
    its tyrants soon or late.
Her pilots flew with Freedom's flag unfurled - on roundel'd
    wings they fought at heaven's gate - the valiant Few -
Against all odds they fought a desperate fight until they
    gained the mastery of the blue;
When Churchill's 'Few' won Freedom in the height -
    remember hippy, brave men died for you.

THE CAUSE

EIGHTY FOUR DAYS was prompted by the praise-worthy attempts of Group Captain Douglas Bader, Lord Boothby and many others to gain somewhat belated but more than deserved recognition for Lord Dowding's inspired conduct of the Battle. An effort was made at the time of the release of the film BATTLE OF BRITAIN to have "Stuffy" Dowding made up to Marshal of the Royal Air Force during his lifetime. Lord Dowding, who was Senior Air Rank Officer at the time of the Battle, received no thanks from authority, and indeed was greatly criticized. Regrettably, Lord Dowding died before the effort to gain him recognition could bear fruit - indeed, if there ever was any chance. But EIGHTY FOUR DAYS, based on the official length of the Battle, was written with some small hope that it might aid his far more eminent champions.

The seeming irreverence occurring in the third verse has root in the code letters 'D.B.' painted on the sides of the illustrious Group Captain's aircraft. They were, of course, his own initials which in audible terms became "Dog's-Body" during Bader's radio contact with his pilots.

--- * ---
*

EIGHTY FOUR DAYS

The eighth day of August was when it began.   The saga
   of eighty-four days.
The conquest of Britain - the "Sealion" plan - had
   entered its first foredoomed phase.
The Nazi Luftwaffe commenced its attack by dive-
   bombing ships in the Channel,
But eight of its Stuka-planes never got back, and this
   marks the start of my annal.
The Battle of Britain chalked up its first score;
In eighty-three days it would add hundreds more.

Goering's pilots were victory-flushed, well-trained and
   attuned for the fight;
The Air-power of Europe lay broken and crushed - and
   this they achieved overnight!
Messerschmitts, Heinkels and Dorniers too, could
   boast a prowess of their own.
Teutonic and masterful these aircraft flew and by
   "super-race" pilots were flown.
Britain's small air force would soon share the plight
Of all that had challenged the Luftwaffe's might.

Be that as it may, and whatever they planned, the
   Luftwaffe's brilliance was clouding,
For over in England at Fighter Command sat a genius
   named "Stuffy" Dowding.
This ingenious Chief was about to bring grief to the
   much-vaunted Nazi Armada;
With his lieutenants lief, he would make its life brief;
   on the eighth it met "Dog's-Body" Bader.
Very soon Marshal Goering had reason to grieve,
For "Stuffy" had many an Ace up his sleeve!

'Johnnie' Johnson, 'Friar' Tuck, were among the great
  Few; 'Sailor' Malan, 'Ginger' Lacey, were too;
Finucane, Rosier, great pilots who, became the Lion's
  claws in the vault of the blue.
These were the Leaders that reached ace-acclaim,
  there were hundreds of heroes unsung;
Men from all nations, too many to name, and some men
  had names I can't tongue.
Here was the "Chicken" that Goering would meet -
That first laid the egg of the Nazi defeat!

Sir Winston Spencer Churchill said, of the pilots that
  fought in the blue,
"Never in human-conflict's field did so many owe much
  to so few."
Before the Battle of Eighty-Four-Days he had promised
  us "blood, sweat, and tears."
"We'll fight on the beaches; we'll fight in the fields;
  if the Nazi invader appears."
"We will never surrender!" Winston said.
The invaders came - as prisoners, or dead!

That glorious summer the Battle was fought ('twas
  glorious weatherwise too),
The Nazi Luftwaffe was near put to naught, by the men
  of the Valiant Few.
There were so many aeroplanes, shattered and bent,
  displaying the Nazi crook-cross;
That no-one took cover when raid-sirens went, for
  everyone knew who was boss!
The Sussex Downs and Orchard Weald of Kent
Received the proud Luftwaffe - wrecked and spent.

EIGHTY FOUR DAYS

Beautiful contrail patterns displayed the embattled
  heights of the blue;
Another decimated raid had been thwarted again by
  the Few.
At first the people watching below would stand in the
  streets and cheer,
And the greatest tribute given the Few, was that nobody
  showed any fear.
At first they scanned the skies whilst engines roared,
Then no-one looked, and some were even bored!

And what a tribute to courage it was; that folk never
  doubted their worth;
The novelty gone from the often-seen sight of a Nazi
  plane plunging to earth.
It was their finest hour; it was our finest hour, for
  the Nation relied on these men.
They were fighting our fight against Germany's might,
  we were solidly purposeful then.
Firing our guns and shooting down Huns they flew
But anyone could die - not just the Few.

The men and women - the children too; all fought in
  the Battle of Britain;
From the valiant pilots that duelled in the skies to the
  child tightly hugging its kitten.
All were the target of enemy planes, their morale
  destroyed was the aim.
A paralysed, panic-torn Britain the prize for the army
  which so nearly came.
The Nation's courage met beyond all praise
The challenge of those four-and-eighty days.

So raise your glass to the pilots who flew and defeated
the Hun in the height;
To Hurricanes and Spitfires too, which served them so
well in the fight.
With our thanks to the man at Fighter Command whose
genius thwarted the Hun;
We salute Lord "Stuffy" Dowding for the marvellous job
that was done.
Montgomery, Lord Alamein won praise.
Dowding, Lord of Four-and-Eighty Days?

THE MEN

Dowding's right hand man throughout the Battle, Keith Park, then Air Vice Marshal, commanded the vital 11 Group of Fighter Command.

Two key factors dictated the geographical course of the Battle: 1. The proximity of the South East corner of England to the French Coast, beyond which was based the massed strength of the Luftwaffe's bombers and fighters. 2. The Messerschmitt 109's limited range of four hundred miles.

The prime task of the Luftwaffe was the destruction of Fighter Command's precious fighters and their air-fields. Inevitably, Park's 11 Group, based in the Home Counties bore the brunt of the Battle, with the bulk of the air fighting taking place over Sussex and Kent. Magic names such as Biggin Hill, West Malling, Hawkinge, Manston, Tangmere, North Weald, Horn-church, and Rochford, literally pinpointed the Battle arena. From these airfields flew the pilots facing the main weight of the Luftwaffe's assault - the men of Park's 11 Group.

History warrants Dowding's overall strategy for the Air Defence as correct and brilliant. And Park's tactical handling of the Fighter Squadrons of RAF Fighter Command will stand forever as a superb feat of defensive generalship.

Immediately after the decisive victory Dowding was retired and Park removed from his command. Two years later Park was sent to hard-pressed Malta. What a blessing! For in this theatre also he proved himself equally brilliant and effective.

Symbolic of Park's great qualities of leadership was his constant contact with his men. Donning a white flying-suit over his Air Marshal's uniform he would climb into a Hurricane to visit and chat with his pilots. There can be no doubt that being led by an active and battle-trained pilot contributed immeasurably to the morale, not only of the Few, but of the gallant band of pilots who saved the critically strategic and devastated George Cross Island of Malta.

———————— *
*
————————

TO THE UNSUNG WARRIOR

The Great War's crude planes etched ugly brown stains
    when men raped the new-conquered height,
And a cordite-sped hell from machine-gun or shell
    tossed them roasting or pulped from the fight.
Regardless of losses the cockades and crosses jinked
    wildly to dodge or deal death;
Their cloth and wood planes singing bracing-wire
    strains, spuming burnt castor oil in hot breath.
And thus they wrote on Nineteen-Eighteen's page
The lessons for a future Battle's rage.

TO THE UNSUNG WARRIOR

In that dogfight tangle there flew from Bertangles a
    pilot who later would spark
Freedom's flame in the blue with an immortal Few,
    Nineteen-Forty sore-needed Keith Park.
Tho' records are written as Battle of Britain,
    it was fought over Sussex and Kent;
Park's Eleven Group band fought the Battle firsthand
    backed by other Groups' fighters when sent.
Their squadrons came to succour his depleted;
No rest for Park, his burdened-days repeated.

When the pressure could spare he'd relinquish his chair
    and fly to each 'drome of his Group
In a lone Hurricane risking combat again he brought
    cheer to his war-weary troop.
At the height of the Battle a Messerschmitt's rattle
    might well have stopped short history's pen,
But the often seen sight of the pilot in white meant the
    Chief was "Up Front" with his men.
New Zealand's son in Britain's hour of need
Inspired the Few with courage, word and deed.

When the Battle was won and its hero unsung was
    assigned with no thanks to save Malta
The Few's revered Chief set about bringing grief
    to the Luftwaffe horde in that quarter.
Again his Spitfires dispatched Nazi-fliers - and many
    Italians, to boot,
Proving Park's tactics right; that he knew how to fight -
    and his young pilots knew how to shoot.
To Malta came a knight when need was stark.
All praise to Air Chief Marshal Sir Keith Park.

Little more than a boy in 1918, Leslie Nixon became the youngest inmate of Germany's notorious Holzminden Lager when the petrol tank of his Sopwith Camel was holed by the German ace, Könnecke.

"Nicco's" later distinctions included the winning of the Sassoon Trophy and the mapping of Cyprus from the air. A DH9 crash in India left him with a permanent scar on his forehead and disaster reached for him again when as Group Captain and Air Officer Commanding Northern Ireland, his beloved Spitfire, 'JP', was threatened with destruction in a thunderstorm over the Irish Sea.

Station Commander of Leconfield, 1940, "Nicco" was always the epitome of an officer and a gentleman. He exuded courage and possessed the gift of clear perception at all times.

---------------- *
---------------- *
*

STATION COMMANDER

My beloved "Nicco" used to 'phone me every day,
"Good mornin', was there somethink, sir?" invariably
   I'd say.
And then we'd chat of all the things that "Nicco" meant
   to me:
A lifelong pilot, RAF, and one-time RFC.
His dogfight days in Camels; Holzminden's prison-cage.
High jinks, which when a subaltern invoked high-
   ranking rage.
Our "Groupie" earned new rank when he retired;
"Himself" to we who loved him and admired.

STATION COMMANDER

But Battle over Britain was a subject of delight
And I've often been much-favoured to discuss it thro'
  the night
With Leconfield's Commander under whom the Poles
  were trained,
And when flung into the Battle became feared as well
  as famed.
"Nicco" flew a famous Spitfire, once the mount of
  Johnny Peel,
Claimed by some as 'first-shot' Spitfire in the Battle's
  early zeal.
Today are left two photos of 'JP'
And on his shelf a model made by me.

The fates were never very kind to "Nicco" thro' his
  life,
Except for meeting Peta, who became his lovely wife.
And tragedy struck hard and fast with two successive
  strokes
To rob him of his speech and limbs - an outrage which
  evokes
Not just a sense of helplessness, but consciousness
  of loss,
No 'phone, nor now "Good mornin', sir," to
  Leconfield's old boss.
So I defy a crippled man with no remorse - you see -
If he could talk, I know he'd say, "Don't you dare
  mention me!"

In virtually every written reference to the Battle of Britain some comparison with the Spanish Armada is made. Constant research as an aviation historian, coupled with a love of the poets, often finds my desk an unlikely mixture of poetic works, aeronautical textbooks, war memoirs and biographies.

A few years ago, whilst researching some writings of Quentin Reynolds, War Correspondent in 1940, in which he referred to Bader's early exploits in the Battle of Britain (in the then present tense), my mind became infused with a somewhat heady mixture of DRAKE'S DRUM by Sir Henry John Newbolt and the previously mentioned accounts of Bader's experiences - DRAKE'S HURRICANE was the result.

———————— * ————————
*

DRAKE'S HURRICANE

Old England lay imperilled under cloudless summer-
skies by the second Great Armada - soon to come.
The Spanish one defeated underneath the Channel lies,
and to the Nation Drake bequeathed his drum;
Saying, "Take this back to England - hang it somewhere
near the sea and bang it if your powder-kegs run short.
Then if I hear it sounding I'll know England's need of me,
so straightway I will quit my heavenly port."

They brought it back to England and they hung it on the
Hoe - to hang in silence nigh four hundred year;
Since he drummed 'em up the Channel - as he did so long
ago - invader's boots had never been so near.
Plymouth knew that he would come - if they tattoo'd on his
drum, so they beat it loud and long in dear old Devon.
In a flash Sir Francis knew he was needed by the Few
for he'd seen this new armada close to heaven.

Having roved the Spanish Main - tacked the Horn and
backed again thro' storm and tempest he had sailed the
"Hind";
So he chose an aeroplane - aptly called a "Hurricane",
and a pilot with a quick and fearless mind.
In its cockpit, cramping small, there was hardly room at
all, but Drake had little need of space to ride;
And he used tin hollow legs as his spirit powder-kegs
to inspire the pilot flying at his side.

16

Nineteen-Forty, August-eight - Goering's hordes attacked
    too late - tho' he boasted as he launched his winged
    armada -
Of the end already fated to befall the Few that waited,
    but in the air were Drake and Douglas Bader!
The Luftwaffe without check would soon "wring the
    Chicken's neck", and then would come the great
    "Sealion" invasion;
But that Chicken had some Peck! - and it very soon made
    wreck of the Nazi dream of England's devastation.

Nineteen-Forty, August-eight - Goering's hordes attacked
    too late, and Bader's voice came through the speaker-
    panel;
He didn't then relate that they had clobbered eight, he
    calmly told them, "It's still Churchill's Channel."
Countless contrails in the blue daily showed the dauntless
    Few, ever-busy decimating the armada;
In the cheering public view - new Elizabethans flew,
    spurred on by Drake in Squadron Leader Bader.

Their squirting leaden-hails smashed the Nazi bent-
    crossed tails or turned their engines into smoking scrap;
Then moaning high-pitched wails - with flame-tipped
    smoking trails, denoted they were caught in Bader's trap.
Among the fields of Kent - smoking, twisted, flaming, bent;
    fell Messerschmitts and Dorniers every day.
To their country graveyards sent by the Few without relent,
    and hundreds of them lined the Pilgrim's Way.

German staffels sadly-mauled, flown by pilots shock-
    appalled, suffered quick-diminished numbers all the way;
Bader's Squadrons - radar-called, talked with plotters at
    their board and were vectored in to pump a deathly spray.

DRAKE'S HURRICANE

If the Nazis made attack - very few would make it back
    for "Dog's-Body" well-organized their slaughter;
Thus, their nerve began to crack - shattered by a 'Hunter-
    pack' that smashed them into ground - or cruel water.

At last the Battle won - "bandits" no more dared to run
    the gauntlet of his pilots seeking prey;
For flying in the sun to the much-avaunted Hun, meant
    Hurricanes and Spitfires in array.
The slip-stream hazy breath of the roundel bearing death
    had put the cross-marked Luftwaffe to flight.
And when the vanquished Hun dare not venture in the sun,
    he sneaked in - like a robber in the night.

It was Winston Churchill who - said in tribute to the Few,
    that in the field of human conflict never
So great a debt was due from so many to so few; then
    he wrote their names in history - forever.
Squadron Leader Bader's legs WERE Drake's spirit
    powder-kegs- and it isn't hard to prove- just ask around!
For whenever Bader flew, he was Admiral of the Few -
    and a bold swashbuckling Leader on the ground.

With one last look at Devon Francis Drake set sail for
    heaven; his England still unconquered kept her Channel.
Some do not believe in heaven - or that Drake came back
    to Devon, and they scorn my humble rhyme of history-
    annal.
But if it be some other foe seeks to lay Old England low -
    don't sit at home and tremble - let him come!
Once the men of Devon know, danger threatens Plymouth
    Hoe - they only need to beat upon Drake's Drum!

Wing Commander Robert Stanford Tuck was not only a top-scoring Ace of the 'Few', he was generally acknowledged to be a perfectionist among them.

Tuck was a professional in comparison with his many volunteer contemporaries.

All wars and critical historical events give birth to legend, and the incredible luck of Stanford Tuck is by no means an exception.

The events depicted here are factual and there is no intention to portray Stanford Tuck in any other light than that of a very brave professional pilot and a very warm humane man.

———————— *
                * ————————

TUCK'S LUCK

Like the stirring sound of a bugle's round bringing
   summons to all but the deaf;
The injunction that found him with thoughts all abound,
   was "Fly with the RAF".
So the gods contrive and the fates connive and a legend
   is born among men;
With the power to arrive and a gift to survive in some
   moment of history when
By hand of fate a blow must-needs be struck -
The gods were weaning Robert Stanford Tuck.

TUCK'S LUCK

Giving heed to command - as the gods had planned -
  he attended his first interview;
Perhaps fate took a hand - how could men understand
  they were choosing an Ace for the Few?
Tho' his parents complained, as a pilot he trained,
  but was not very good at the start;
And his confidence waned as he struggled and strained
  in his efforts to master the art.
Concern for his career began to grow -
The fates just smiled - and ruled what would be so.

So they persevered as the tumult neared with its
  dictator-swaggering dawn;
Whilst the Nazis cheered and the Fascists jeered their
  prince of the Few was born.
At the gods' behest with his courage and zest he was
  groomed for his reign in the height;
And in resolute quest he prepared for the test of his
  great but yet undreamed-of fight.
In war-torn skies no better pilot flew -
The great perfectionist among the Few.

With his task unfulfilled Tuck would never be killed, for
  the fates would support their decisions;
In his role he'd been skilled for a future they willed -
  thus he lived twice thro' mid-air collisions!
With a scarring-weal they set the seal of the duellist
  upon his right cheek;
And opponents would reel from his musketeer-zeal
  when its prowess was sharpened to peak.
The gods had made a knight to fight the hordes
Whilst Camm and Mitchell forged his duelling-swords.

In the smoke-pall murk over doomed Dunkerque he
    encountered his first Messerschmitt,
And by some strange quirk as he went to work it
    zoomed up into cloud and then quit.
Then the Nazi-flier having dodged the Spitfire levelled-
    out and set course for his base;
In consequence dire he was riddled by fire from the
    guns of a resolute Ace.
And so it was that Tuck commenced a score
Destined to add another thirty-four.

Of the Battle of Britain so much has been written -
    and some I have rendered in verse;
Of the Luftwaffe smitten - its fliers ground-bitten - of
    flaming destruction and worse.
But the story of Tuck - and especially his luck - would
    take volumes and oceans of time;
So admiring his pluck and the blows that he struck I
    will limit the scope of my rhyme
To brief appraisal of this fearless Ace
With skill and courage that outlived the pace.

In a tavern one night via some second sight he finished
    his glass and then went;
For persuade as he might all his comrades sat tight
    and he couldn't explain what he meant.
That night he had been at the old Ferry Inn and just as
    "Last orders!" were called
A bomb-blasting din smashed the old tavern in and the
    news of it left him appalled.
Premonition? - Psychic second-sight?
The gods had plucked their chosen from his plight!

TUCK'S LUCK

In the words of the Psalm he could not come to harm
  tho' a thousand should fall at his side;
And the gods without qualm saved their chosen right-
  arm altho' thousands of others had died.
From a Spitfire ablaze and with hardly a graze he had
  baled-out on several occasions;
And tracer-streamed rays smashed his canopy-glaze
  but his body defied their invasions.
His throttle-lever blown from out his hand,
His thigh immune by penny-armour spanned!

He remembers well being saved by the bell of a last-
  minute telephone-call;
For he cursed like hell at the airman's yell in reluctance
  to answer at all.
To avoid overheat he relinquished the seat of the
  Typhoon awaiting its test -
Dumped his 'chute at his feet as he beat a retreat to
  his office then talked to the 'pest'.
The fume-filled Typhoon crashed a mile away -
And yet again Tuck's luck had ruled the day!

Now there's nothing worse than a lengthy verse so I
  promise to finish it soon;
I would like to be terse but my subject's adverse - I
  might just as well spit at the moon.
The incredible luck of the immortal Tuck played a
  prominent part, none-the-less,
It mustn't detract from the plain simple fact he was
  brilliant and brave under stress.
Precision-like and deadly when he flew -
A man of many parts - resourceful, too.

His luck served him most just beyond the French coast
    when his Merlin was silenced by flak;
And his enemy-host was denied of the boast that he'd
    fallen in dogfight attack.
There seemed nowhere to hand where his Spitfire could
    land and a flak-truck took shots at him still;
But the gods had it planned and his finale-grand was to
    make that flak-truck his last kill!
Defiant with its belly near the ground
The dying Spitfire's guns their target found.

From the impact he flinched - he was bound to be
    lynched - even if he climbed out of the wreck;
But his fate had been clinched as he skilfully inched
    the Spit to its ground-hugging check.
The Germans aghast from his accurate blast viewed the
    scene where their slain comrades lay;
Their shooting outclassed by the plane that lay grassed -
    the Spitfire a few yards away.
One shell went down the barrel of their gun!
A feat applauded even by the Hun!

As from every scrape he was sure to escape and his
    fortunes were naturally legion.
In the blood-stained drape of a bullet-holed cape he
    traversed a snow-covered region;
On the Russian Front he was caught in the brunt of a
    battle that threatened his life.
The Russians were blunt in their thirst for the hunt and
    they kept him with them in the strife.
Deserting them he trekked upon his way -
But luck had yet another part to play!

TUCK'S LUCK

With a grizzled frown in a Polish town he pondered on
    what to do next;
For a Russian-clown clad in bear-fur brown was his
    shadow with little pretext.
At the height of his fear to his startled ear there came
    a Cockney greeting!
And for many a year he would almost cheer at the
    thought of that fantastic meeting!
"Wotcher Guv! - Ain't yore name Stanford Tuck?"
Tuck's senses reeled as he stood thunderstruck!

"You won't know me - an' it's all Q. T. - I was 'long of
    yore bruvver Jack -
We was captured d'ye see - very close to the sea -
    outside Calais as matterafack.
So 'ave no fear - 'cos now yore 'ere me missus'll soon
    get you right;
But please get it clear - folks at 'ome mustn't 'ear 'cos
    they fink I got killed in the fight......."
So Tuck was led to safety by the gods -
Or would the doubters calculate the odds?

There is much more to tell but I think it is well that
    I make this the end of my rhyme;
He survived shot and shell, trudged a snowy-waste hell,
    and his luck saw him through every time -
And before I forget I haven't said yet that they once
    fished him out of the Channel!
He was more than an Ace with a duellist-grace. He's
    the legend that spices the annal!
To Wing Commander Robert Stanford Tuck
My humble rhyme - and very best of luck!

When Barry Winchester told me that he wished to use my name in the dedication of his book EIGHTY FOUR DAYS, it was with a great sense of pride and privilege that I realised I was being invited to represent all those aircrew who flew and fought in the Battle of Britain.

We were, of course, the fortunate few: those who by the luck of the draw or by some kind twist of fate were posted at the completion of their training to a Fighter Squadron. At least, therefore, we had at our disposal first-class, well-armed, competitive equipment. If ever there was a chance to give good account, it must surely have been under such circumstances.

Many were less fortunate than we. They would have given anything for the same opportunity. As it was, their courage and devotion, often displayed in obsolete aircraft, were awe-inspiring to any company and their bravery could not have been surpassed.

If one must fight a war, then many will pay the extreme sacrifice. Those of the 'Few' who did not return were lost doing something they prized dearly above all else:- flying in defence of their homeland, Freedom, or both, against an utterly ruthless enemy invader, and piloting Spitfires and Hurricanes of Fighter Command, Royal Air Force.

6. 11. 73   GEOFFREY WELLUM

TO SQUADRON LEADER GEOFFREY WELLUM, DFC*

How privileged I am to see in you
The sacred living flame of Churchill's 'Few';
A knight who rode immortal Spitfire wings
In deadly joustings o'er our realm of kings,
To keep for me the Gate of Freedom's Right,
And pledged his life so tho' he fell I might
Hold fast in turn the heritage that he,
With every pilot in his company,
Prized dear above such ghastly sacrifice
As carbon'd flesh or plummet's pulping price.
Upon that Battle's rage Time heaps its years
And in my hand today, mute souvenirs
Impute their hallowed meaning to my grasp;
His priceless Battle over Britain Clasp;
Reflected in his Flying Cross I see
A now far-off September day when he
Contested hated Heinkels o'er my head -
I rode my grocer's-cycle whilst he sped
In sleek avenging Spitfire thro' the sky
(Tho' only glinting wings could I descry)
To use it like some fine steel-tempered sword
Designed to decimate the Nazi horde.
But that was long before I ever wrote
Of one, who altho' then was so remote,
With whom I flew and fought in boyish mind
And met in later years which have combined
To burden me with estimate of worth.
For who dares value pricelessness on earth?
So then this verse in place of estimation,
To Geoff, with all my fondest admiration.

* Flying Officer with 92 Squadron, Biggin Hill

The story of how the 'Seven Sons of Uncle Sam' arrived in England to fly with the RAF would make a volume in its own right and their courage and sacrifice are beyond praise, therefore, may this verse suffice.

—————— * ——————
*

EAGLE SQUADRON

Seven Sons of Uncle Sam have special mention
   right;
For long before their country saw the tumult as
   its fight
They looked upon this England as the Mother
   of the Free;
Cajoled, connived, conspired, contrived, until
   remarkably,
From peace and plenty USA they reached our
   war-torn shore,
Avowed allegiance to our King and his
   commission bore.
Did Georgie Washington turn in his grave -
Or did he recognise the lead they gave?

Which case was so, we'll never know, but this
    magnificent seven
Extolled his Torch of Liberty thro' all the
    heights of heaven.
"Red" Tobin, Pilot Officer, was one of our
    great 'Few',
Along with "Andy" Mamedoff and A. G.
    Donahue.
"Shorty" Keogh, Haviland, Leckrone and
    "Billy" Fiske
All fought and flew in Air Force blue when
    Freedom was at risk.
With names that with a Western well compare
These 'cowboys' fought their gun-fights in the air.

So young and gay, what need had they for little
    recompense -
Give one life in the Battle, then five more in
    our defence?
Magnificent their sacrifice, inadequate our
    praise,
But ours is now their kingdom, may the land
    that gave them raise,
Remember Sons we honour here who knew
    above all things
That Freedom's Right transcends the laws of
    Presidents or Kings.
America, may you be proud as we
Of these the vanguard of your destiny.

Traditionally, from early Royal Flying Corps days, fighter pilots have worn their tunics with the top button left undone to distinguish them from other operational pilots.

———————— * ————————
*

FIGHTER PILOT

Among the King's tall warriors, a
   stripling;
Drake's buccaneers, Royal Henry's
   bowmen true,
Preserved his race: he battles in the
   skies
More trained and skilled than tar or
   soldier born,
Encapsuled with his weapons; set apart,
Anonymous, remotely: a coloured number
   crackling on the unseen ether,
Valhalla echoing while valkyries ponder;
His pirouettes and wildly dodging jinks;
His trigger-stuttered streams of fiery
   darts;
The flashing metal wings that bear him
   up
Thro' depthless dizzy canyons in the
   towering cliffs of cloud;

FIGHTER PILOT

Wreathing, shifting, temporal walls of
    Death's Arena.
This valiant jousting knight of high-borne
    yeomanry,
Whose vapoured pennon blazons English
    skies
With heraldry of Freedom's Resolution,
Walks in the crowd: his topmost tunic
    button left undone.

Based on a related episode which I thought worth recording.

———— * ————
*

THIRTY YEARS ON

At London Airport the other week, I met "Revs" Barratt
    of Four-six-two;
When the Battle of Britain was at its peak, he was one
    of the valiant 'Few'.
He shouted down from the waving-base - having seen
    some relatives off;
"Hey! Treacle! There's no need to race - come up
    and I'll order some scoff."

We went to the restaurant - ordered a drink - and
    nattered of days gone by;
"Revs" looked at Eileen - gave her a wink - then said
    "Do you still let him fly?"
Eileen smiled across at me - "You try to stop him!"
    she said;
"Fancy flying at ninety-three - he's still a bit light in
    the head!"

THIRTY YEARS ON

The same old "Revs" - he hadn't changed, and nobody
  eyeing him knew;
That in the gathering fate had arranged, sat one of the
  valiant 'Few'.
My young co-pilot joined the group, and tho' only
  twenty-two;
He was almost as thrilled as a child with a hoop to be
  talking to one of the 'Few'.

Don't you wish you were flying again?" he asked as
  "Revs" pondered his gin;
"Revs" gave him a look of injured-pain, and then he
  replied with a grin.
"I have no wish to push my luck! - I've had a few shaves
  in the air!
Sometimes I do - if I'd still have the pluck - but I've
  got that I don't really care. "

"When I think how often I've had a scare that left me
  sweating with fear;
I'd rather be here - wishing I was up there, than up
  there wishing I was down here! "
I'm glad I met old "Revs" again - he's the most modest
  pilot I knew;
He knocked down six in his Hurricane, and is typically
  one of the 'Few'.

Who else but a man who experienced the Battle first-hand could write a truly accurate and vivid account of one of the many dogfights that were a daily occurrence on the London scene of 1940?

The short answer is 'nobody', and the surviving heroes of that gallant band who were Churchill's 'Few' seem to be conversant on all other subjects but that of personal valour.

With some technical knowledge and personal flying experience, it was felt that an attempt at a dogfight episode should be made in this volume. Therefore, supplementing meagre qualification and imagination with an outline of battle experience in another field and another era, SERGEANT PILOT is inspired by WOUNDED, the work of a favourite poet, Robert W. E. Service.

——————— * ———————
*

SERGEANT PILOT

Who would believe?   Some eighteen months ago,
With little thought beyond each passing day,
I drove a London bus from Walthamstow,
Was reasonably happy, I would say.
Yes, with my little world I was content,
Enjoying life that ran a smoothish round
Of bustling miles in stop-start driving spent;
Of happy hours with girls or friends I found.

33

SERGEANT PILOT

Our world revolved around our football team,
And raising funds to meet the old folks'needs;
Then bang! A bloke called Hitler breaks my dream -
I'm flashing thro' the sky at breathless speeds.
My eager Spitfire carries me to War:
Me, the bloke that drove a bus before.

More weird than any film I ever saw;
I hurtle thro' this battle in the sky,
With snarling Merlin revving at full bore;
The pounding stops and tracer flashes by.
Hit in the leg! - but can't be much at all;
Thank God, there's not much damage to the Spit.
I'm strangely calm and feeling ten feet tall,
Exhilarated by the thrill of it.
One Nazi plunging to the ground is mine,
My guns have sent him vanquished from the fight;
Now if I die I have no cause to whine,
At least I've struck a blow in Freedom's Right.
That Messerschmitt near clobbered me for fair,
'Twas my good luck that Leader saw him there.

My leg hurts now, I feel it growing stiff;
Yet in the fight a bullet merely stings;
You don't feel much, it hits you with a biff,
But you're too busy dodging flashing wings.
Fly For Your Life!   As other aircraft fall;
A hard-pressed Spitfire weaves and jinks like mad;
You dive to help, too late!   No Spit at all -
You hope to hell he hasn't copped it bad.
Fly For Your Life!   The sky is spewing death,
And smoking trails that blossom all around.

34

At any second death may claim your breath,
And send you plunging lifeless to the ground.
Fly For Your Life! How strange to have no fear!
Machine-gun tracer flicks across your path;
Another Spit whangs by - collision-near,
A Heinkel flames, the skies are full of wrath.
Fly For Your Life! You chase your quarry down;
His cowling splashes light beneath your blast;
An oil-slick stains the sky a dirty-brown;
A parachute! - You've got your Hun at last!
You stick hard back. The ground is straight ahead.
Climb For Your Life! The earth tilts out of view;
A Heinkel waffles past - its pilot dead.
(Your leg is hurting now - that worries you).
You scan the sky. You think you are alone.
But no! Another Heinkel losing height;
A straggler badly hit and on his own,
With smoking engine damaged in the fight.
Christ! - Here's another Hun - just like the first,
Although, perhaps more of a sitting-duck;
You line him up and get him with one burst;
A nifty shooting job, but mainly luck.
See any more? Let's find another Hun.
Climb For Your Pay! And to the battle-brink;
Your blasted leg! It seems to weigh a ton;
And what you'd give if you could get a drink.
A group of tracer zips across your wing;
Some Messerschmitt is closing for a kill!
You jink away - but cannot see a thing -
He overshoots - his guns are firing still.
Your leg is dripping blood - you're seeing red;
You're battle-mad - you have the bastard now;

SERGEANT PILOT

A quick manoeuvre puts him dead ahead -
He falls in bits - you got him anyhow.
Your leg's too stiff, you cannot hold the turn
And down you go - perhaps it saves your life.
You nearly hit a Heinkel's flaming-burn
That hurtles down in plummet from the strife.
You gasp, you cower; then once again you plunge;
A crazy melee, whilst the whole world reels.
Shoot For Your Life! You jink, you roll, you lunge;
With other Spitfires chasing at their heels.
The taste of triumph. . . . then you're feeling queer. . . .
That blasted leg! It kills you, bloody near.

Both wars bred heroes of a very special kind - night-fliers. In World War 1, the famous ace, "Billy" Bishop, VC, described his short spell in the game. "It was like being dumped into an unknown lake at night." In World War 11, when the Luftwaffe resorted to its night-terror Blitz, speeds of aircraft had risen to a point where ill-equipped pilots stood precious chance of finding elusive targets. Nevertheless, many brave men accepted the perilous challenge, and although success eluded the stalwarts of 1940, radar eventually provided the answer along with specialised aircraft such as the Beaufighter. Two pilots who won great renown were Flight Lieutenant John "Cat's eyes" Cunningham, CBE, DSO, DFC, and Squadron Leader Max Aitken, DSO, DFC, MP, son of Lord Beaverbrook.

---------------- * ----------------
*

NIGHTFIGHTERS

The first night-skulking raiders were the Kaiser's
　Zeppelins, Leviathans of Death in English skies.
With Leefe Robinson of Cuffley earning VC fame, begins
　our page of dauntless pilots forced to rise
On flimsy wings to awesome heights with little else but
　faith and courage of a very special kind
To challenge instruments of dark, aloof to night cloud
　wraith, of a fearless foe with skilful-cunning mind.

NIGHTFIGHTERS

They were blind men on a cliff-face seeking eagles in
   the night, yet they faced such peril with impunity.
Thro' months of sour frustration groping up to reach
   the height affording mocking foes immunity.
But they won thro' with dogged guts and duty's firm
   resolve, igniting gas-borne giants with tiny sparks,
To watch their fiery tumble in horrific heat's dissolve,
   as Sowrey, Tempest, Pyott, made their marks.

Yet nameless unsung heroes took with these an equal
   chance; some crashed and died with little gain to
   show.
Their efforts found no lauding nor were crowned with
   Fame's romance, along with me but few their names
   still know.
And so in Nineteen-Forty's fight the game remained
   the same - if anything the risks were greater yet
Defiants, Spits, and Hurricanes upheld that sacred
   flame till Cunningham and Aitken paid the debt.

When Churchill conferred immortality on the word
'Few' he used it to portray the extent of the indebtedness
of the many.   Lest in the mists of time the public image
of the 'Few' should dim to the point of being vague, an
attempt to identify them is included.

----------- * -----------
*

HOW MANY WERE THE FEW

They came from many nations, the men of the valiant
  'Few',
Twenty-five-hundred British; Australians, twenty-two.
A hundred from New Zealand; from Canada, ninety-
  four;
Ten fighting men from Erin's Isle; South Africa, a
  score.
A hundred plus from Poland; another ninety Czech;
Thirty Belgian; fourteen French; to save the "Chicken's"
  neck.
Seven sons of Uncle Sam; from Israel came one;
Another from Jamaica, with one Rhodesian.
Three thousand gallant pilots to fight the Nazi hordes,
With courage far beyond the praise of languages and
  words.
A thousand suffered burns and wounds; five hundred
  gave their lives.
And in the hearts of all free men their memory survives.

THE PLOT

The fantastic volume and variety of information arriving at Fighter Command Headquarters, Bentley Priory, played a vital role in the Battle. Such information came from a number of sources to pass through the Filter Rooms until the Controllers were enabled to build a comprehensive plot of all that was happening. Not only did the various organizations contribute to the plots, but were themselves fed back with the results derived. Thus, the Police were 'in the picture' and could issue air raid warnings and alerts to both the Public and all civilian organizations. This whole operation could truly be described as a grand conspiracy.

--- * ---
*

THE PLOTTERS

Girls in blue-grey playing some sort of war-game;
Smart in their uniforms, hair neatly done.
Feminine frownings o'er grid map in table frame,
Cueing hued counters with no sense of fun.

Men round a gallery, stern-faced as umpires,
'Phoning terse commentaries, heaven knows where.
One girl's deft move sending squadrons of Spitfires
Up to give battle miles high in the air.

Telephones, microphones, lined-up in batteries;
Signal-boards wink like pin-table displays;
Men speak to girls using terms far from flatteries;
Headphones clamp hair in unglamorous ways.

Pretty brunette sprouting mouthpiece from shirted-
    breasts;
Grim capless pilot flies proxy by 'phone
Making decisions which all in his charge invests,
Voice leading pilots where he's never flown.

Here the nerve centre of all Britain's Home Defence;
Pilots and policemen, observers and tars,
Soldiers and firemen and Air Raid Precautions, whence
Comes grand conspiracy, dictate of Mars.

THE MACHINES

The fantastic achievements of Lord Beaverbrook and his role in the Battle have been dealt with in detail in many books.   This humble tribute to a great man makes no pretence of knowing how he did it - what matters is that somehow he did!

*
*

EAGER BEAVER

Where did those Spitfires come from?
Their Hurricane partner-planes, too?
They still fought when Goering had reckoned
His Air Force had flattened our few.
He must have thought Dowding had access
To some kind of conjuring hat
From which he pulled fighters like rabbits -
And he wasn't far-out at that!
From Canada came our magician
Who scorned doing things by the book,
And we fought a war of attrition
By God's Grace and Lord Beaverbrook!

Perhaps in common with the public of those historic days, I have fallen for the magic trap into which the name SPITFIRE would seem to lure writers. The elliptical beauty of line, almost comparable to that of a ballerina, gave the Spit a distinct advantage in a concours d'elegance with its equally essential contemporary in the Battle of Britain, the Hawker Hurricane. As things worked out, Camm's Hurricane, which greatly outnumbered Mitchell's Spitfire used in the Battle, was ideally suited for dealing with the bomber hordes, due to its rugged construction and ability to withstand considerable punishment from the bomber's crossfire. However, the Spitfire, being more nimble than its counterpart, largely dealt with the German fighter cover and was perhaps even more preciously regarded than the Hurricane, if for no other reason than its lack of numbers.

———————— * ————————
*

SPITFIRE

The Spitfire claws thro' the cumulus clouds on elliptical
    rime-dulled wings
Which buffet and sway thro' the yielding shrouds as
    the bellowing Merlin sings
And chases the whirling spinner-cone as threshing
    prop bores on
Up where no feathered-wing has flown to trill its joyous
    song.
Thro' streaming perspex suffused-light grows brighter
    with the pace,
Till roundel'd wings by mirk abused shake off the
    veiled embrace.
Flashing clear in the brilliant sun they cleave the clouds
    asunder;
The muffled depths at last outrun and scorned by the
    Merlin's thunder.

Triumphant in its speeding climb the Spitfire with
    begoggled knight
Becomes the metal-bird sublime conceived by
    Mitchell's saving sight.
Scanning the ceiling-blue of space its shadow flits the
    fleece-cloud floor,
Then wheeling with a gull-like grace the gun-wing
    warrior goes to war.
Soaring high in effortless flight, concealed by a
    pitiless sun,
It waits till a distant glint gives sight and marks the
    intruder-Hun.
Slicing down the awesome height the fighter swoops
    to attack
With bullet-hail scoring in splashes of light as the
    Dornier rolls on its back.

SPITFIRE

Then - only the wide and lonely sky - in seconds it's
    over and done,
With an oil-black plume that drifts on high to show
    where the Dornier spun.
The Spitfire descends thro' the merciless clouds on
    elliptical death-dealing wings,
That buffet and sway thro' the yielding shrouds while
    the Merlin softly sings.

One of my most vivid recollections of the German assault on England in 1940 was the constant aggressive growl of Nazi bombers.

———————— ⁕ ————————
⁕

ON THIN AIR

Goering's glinting gaggles gambit growling in the sky;
Hump-back Hurricanes are spraying death.
Girthed and goggled grim-faced knights ride jousting-
     wings miles high
With sun-seared gaze and oxy-bottled breath.
Shadow shift and counter; frantic weave and jink; men
     and metal torn in anguished fight.
Eagles etching vapour-trails or scrawls in oil-smudge
     ink,
A Tournament for Freedom in the height.
Britain's life hangs thinly in the blue
Dependent on her brave and dauntless 'Few'.

Early Junkers Ju 87A-1s and B-1s proved highly successful in their sinister role during the Spanish Civil War of the late Thirties. Stukas formed the spearhead of Blitzkrieg in Europe and were virtually its symbol. In actual fact, the Stukas' reputation had begun its decline at the time of Dunkirk, but its Waterloo came in 1940's Battle. Unable to survive over England, it suffered appalling losses before being withdrawn.

——————— * ———————
*

JUNKERS 87

Nazi Kultur bred a vulture,
Stuka was its name.
Crook-crank wings bore dive-bomb stings
To hasten Europe's shame.
Nazi Pride jeered those who died
And sent flocked birds of prey
To breed in nests of those oppressed,
As cuckoos will for aye.
Then Dunkirk's beach reviled the screech
Each hideous plummet swelled.
Notorious!   Victorious!
They then sought nests where dwelled
Cockney sparrows o'er the Narrows,
Just a hop from France.
Beyond all words those tiny birds
Led vultures such a dance,
That Stukas came and died of shame
This side of England's Channel.
Thus birds of feather ended tether
Infamous in annal.

A commonplace sight throughout the long summer days of the Battle was that of Messerschmitt 109 fighters which had successfully force-landed. In cornfields and meadows of Essex, Sussex and the Kentish Weald, these gaily painted, neat little aeroplanes could be seen guarded by soldiers as they forlornly awaited the attention of experts from the Royal Air Force. Most of their number were transported to prominent sites in towns and cities where they were displayed to the ever-curious public who willingly gave pennies and small change to Spitfire Funds for the privilege of clambering over the spoils of the air-war being fought over their heads.

Technically, the Messerschmitt 109 was a master-piece of aeronautical engineering. It was surprisingly small for an aircraft which had earned such a big reputation, and the paint schemes of yellow, red, white or blue noses with 'helblau' undersides, coupled with highly coloured markings and motives, afforded the many 'cast-outs' of the Battle a deceptive impression of beauty which belied their lethal capabilities.

As has been stated in other contexts, the fuel capacity of the 109s played a critical role in the events of 1940 and many pilots force-landed aircraft which simply had not sufficient fuel for making the return Channel crossing. More crash-landed on the French beaches for this reason than will ever be known, while countless scores flopped powerless onto the waves and sank silently into the 'ditch'.

———————— * ————————
*

IN A CORNFIELD

There's a Messerschmitt down in the cornfield,
  propeller blades twisted and bent;
Sleek cowling rip-shattered by bullets and frail wings
  all crumpled and rent.
The flaxen-haired youngster who flew it looked shocked
  as they led him away;
But one day he'll laugh with his mother, whilst some
  of his comrades today
Are Goering's slain and gruesome where they dived.
With luck-kissed skill he pancaked and survived.

The dapple-hue plane in the cornfield seems harmlessly
  small and forlorn;
With powder-blue fuselage belly all oil-streaked and
  stone-scored and torn.
Such beauty belies the grim purpose for which it to
  England was sent;
For crosses of Hitler's Luftwaffe emblazon an evil
  intent.
And admiration for this aeroplane
Dissolves at glimpse of crook-swastika stain.

THE TRAGEDY

The Battle of Britain was not purely a matter of airmen fighting for the mastery of the English skies. Let it never be forgotten that however the intellectuals may attempt to pussy-foot the pedal of reality, the Luftwaffe's assault on England was a concept of total and merciless war. The metal missiles tumbling from German bomb bays were designed to be lethal and, make no mistake, they were. The stark violence unleashed on London's sprawling suburbs brought literal massacre to usually the poorest of the populace. Old men, young men; wives and widows; children and babies; all were hideously pulped and maimed in the holocaust of Goering's hoped-for triumph.

--- * ---
*

A CHILD IN THE MIDST

The little girl clutched-tight her severed arm - they'd
  found her searching for it in the muck;
Her parents lay beyond all further harm amid the debris
  where the bomb had struck.
The surgeon gagged to see the gruesome limb -
  demanding why such thing had been allowed;
The child insisted she brought it to him - the Rescue-
  man that held her sobbed aloud.
The surgeon laid her down and stroked her head then
  gently prised the horror from her hand;
"They sewed my Teddy's arm back once," she said -
  the surgeon wept and wished he had a wand.

The hard core of the 'Few' was a precious number of professional pilots. War-time volunteers and auxiliary pilots depended upon the experienced men for leadership. Alas, the ranks of the professionals were depleted in the Battle of France, and as the Battle of Britain took its toll, a great number of young and inexperienced pilots, some with less than twenty hours on Spitfires, took their place in the sore-pressed squadrons. Many failed to return from their first operational sortie.

————— * —————
*

THE SPROG

A flying-log;
Embroidered wings;
The nickname "Sprog"
Scrawled on his things.

He yearned to fly;
Loved aeroplanes;
A magic passion
Coursed his veins.

And so he flew;
In dogfight fell;
Collision slew
His foe as well.

In battle lore,
Aware he lacked;
Made final score
When first attacked.

Beneath the tide
Rests Freedom's Price,
His youth belied
Such sacrifice.

As an ex-Merchant Navy officer I am proud of our traditional title, "The Silent Service". But I am sure all seamen will agree that there is no more silent or forgotten a service than that given to the world's mariners by the courageous men of Trinity House. As this is read hundreds of men are keeping their lonely vigil in a host of Light Vessels and Lighthouses around our entire coastline.

Back in the days of 1940 the above statement was equally valid. The lights were not shown in wartime but all vessels and houses were manned and marked hazards to shipping visually and by audible warning.

The casualty list of Trinity House personnel and property dates from 9th January 1940 to the 18th August 1944. No less than 39 aerial attacks on Light Vessels and Lighthouses are recorded - the last five of which were flying bomb (V.1.) incidents. Lighthouse and Light Vessel personnel were killed and wounded. And Trinity House, Tower Hill, London, was gutted in a fire-bomb raid on the night of 29th December 1940.

During the Battle of Britain the major victim would seem to have been the South Folkestone Gate Light Vessel which the Luftwaffe bombed on the 14th August 1940. The vessel was severely damaged and several men were killed and wounded. No less than 13 Light Vessels were lost during the course of the War. And no plight could have been more helpless than that of their crews. Incapable of manoeuvre, the souls aboard had to take anything that was hurled at them.

The men of the Royal National Lifeboat Institution supplemented the somewhat inadequate Air Sea Rescue Service to a very marked degree. And many airmen

of both sides owe their lives to the lifeboat crews of
1940 who maintained superbly the magnificent traditions
of their calling to the same extent as we still take for
granted today. In war and peace these men are everyday heroes of a very special sort. It is impossible to
praise them enough but mention them I have.

——————— * ———————
*

LIFEBOATS AND LIGHTSHIPS

Brave men in Trinity Lightships;
Heroes of R. N. L. I.
Held fast to their perilous calling
Despite daily threats in the sky.
Their peacetime role essential still
   in war;
The lifeboats rescued airmen by the
   score.

Imagine a powerless lightship
Moored fast on a bank by its chains,
Unarmed in its errand of mercy,
Yet dive-bombed by Luftwaffe planes.
As lifeboats plucked downed Nazis
   from their plight
The Germans slew our men who
   "kept the light".

Based on fact, the narrative seeks to demonstrate how the great spirit of unity which, transcendent in War, continues to survive throughout its aftermath in those rendered dependent one upon another, regardless of rank, by its merciless ravage.

——————— *
          * ———————

THE BROTHERS

I push 'im in this wheelchair an' I
    finds it 'ard ter twig
That they gave 'im orl them medals,
    yet now no-one gives a fig,
As ter 'ow 'e is, or 'ow 'e feels,
    s'long as their orlright
An' anyways, 'is pore burnt mug
    ain't quite a pretty sight.

A flippin' Wing Commander, mate,
    that's wot 'e used ter be
An' now the only pal 'e 'as - a daft
    ole dunce like me.
Me sister she was posh, like, an'
    they married in the War,
Which was 'ow she made us bruvvers -
    least, accordin' ter the law.

THE BROTHERS

Bruvvers? Well, I arsks yer? Me
   an' 'im?   Like chalk an' cheese!
We never 'ardly spoke much, 'til I 'ad
   sum kinda weeze
That 'er an' 'im was betta orf ter live
   at 'ome wiv me
So's I could 'elp look arter 'im - least-
   ways, ter sum degree.

Pore sod!   It orften makes me weep
   rememb'rin' wot 'e was,
Orl lah-di-dah an' wizzo prank - she
   worships 'im becos
'E made 'er verry proud of 'im orl
   gay an' debbonhair,
An' flyin' them there 'Urricanes in
   dawgfights right up there.

Distingwished Servis Order, mate,
   two bars, an' Flyin' Crorse.
We orl goes up the Pallis; cheered
   the King 'til we wos 'orse;
An' spent the night in Lester Square,
   a most unlikely crowd.
'Bout all we 'ad in common was the
   bleedin' blackout shroud!

THE BROTHERS

B'then 'e'd 'ad a fair ole run, an' got
   'is sevenf Fritz.
I 'spose that must've bin the time ole
   Jerry tried 'is Blitz.
'E came 'ome wiv sum pilots an' that
   caused a proper stir
'Cos 'e tells 'em I'm 'is bruvver, an'
   they starts ter corl me, 'Sir!'

Oh, Gawd! I orften chuckle wen I
   finks abart that night.
I couldn't 'old a candle to them boys
   wot fit that fight!
"Yew corl me 'Alf'," I sez to 'em,
   "I'm in the ARP,
The Forses won't at any price take-on
   the likes o' me! "

Well, anyrate, that makes 'em larf an'
   fings went orf quite well.
Until them ruddy sireens go an' Fritz
   starts - Bloody 'ell!
That ain't wot I was tellin' yer, where
   was I? Let me see.....
O'corse, now I remember, 'bout me
   sister's bloke an' me.

Yerse! Beginnin' of October, 'bout
   the Battle's blinkin' end.
We gits this urgent teleegraff, the
   Air Forse used ter send.
I daresn't show me sister so I tells
   a littel fib.
"'E can't be bad, " I sez to 'er, "'E's
   likely cracked a rib. "

No use ter flannel 'er, y'know, she
   gessed it straightaway.
She rushes orf an' goes ter 'im; ten
   days an' she was grey.
"Oh, Alf, " she cries, wen she gits
   back, "They say 'is face is gone. "
"Don't fuss, ole girl, I've orften read
   wot miricles they've done. "

But Graham got no miricle, as you can
   see terday.
'Is back was broke, 'is foot blown 'orf,
   'is face orl burnt away.
'E gits jumped be sum Meshersmit wot
   sets 'is plane alight
An' be the time as 'e gits out 'e's in
   a sorry plight.

THE BROTHERS

Wiv parashoot a-smoulder an' 'is
  body one big blister,
They dunno 'ow 'e lived, ole mate, it
  nearly kills me sister.
So anyway, that's 'ow it was, an' 'ow
  comes 'e's wiv me.
I luvs 'im like a bruvver, an' it's
  mewchewal, d'yer see?

Yet even arter orl o' that, 'e lives
  fer airyplanes.
I'd take a proper int'rest too, if I 'ad
  'arf 'is brains.
But we've 'ad a lot in common since
  that buzz-bomb near-croaked me,
'Cos I got our legs fer walkin' - an'
  'e's got our eyes ter see.

The Luftwaffe's merciless assault on our cities, London in particular, was a frightful and seemingly never-ending experience which once undergone can never be forgotten. But Goering's night-terror Blitz is beyond all description. Entire families vanished in a blinding instant that has left others maimed for ever. Whole blocks of humble streets, still familiar and beloved at dusk, had appeared in the dust-choked dawn as mind-boggling slag-heaps created by unseen maniacal demons during the sleepless night's spell. There are no words for our fears and apprehensions of that time and my own family is left with thankful memories of our deliverance whilst still possessing souvenirs which forcibly remind us, in an uncaring age, of the stark reality of what even we sometimes find hard to believe was more than a ghastly nightmare.

———————— * ————————
*

BLITZED

My Aunt, whom all my years adore,
I almost lost in time of war
When Heinkel bombs spaced Death's grim spore
Along the street where she
And Uncle kept my birthplace home,
Till separate of Time and foam
Took him to Italy.

BLITZED

Bright windows of my childhood sight
Thro' which I watched lamplighters light
Gas beacon posts to cheer the night
Dissolved in death-sheen dust.
Encrusting frames and ancient door
It glittered as some Hell-frost hoar
Bequeathed from Satan's trust.

Loved brickwork stared with glazeless sash,
Stark weals of splintered fragment slash,
On Devil dust-pyred priceless trash
Reduced to piled debris.
As shredded drapes flapped by a breeze
Made stricken signals of disease
Which morons flock to see.

Good neighbours died in instant flare,
Or under mounds in pained despair,
By hands unseen in night-cloaked air
At maniac behest.
Yet still my Aunt is living there
In house retrieved by skilled repair.
My Uncle now at rest.

To Doris and my Uncle 'Son',
Whose memory lives while these lines run,
This place in rhymes of Battle won
To show how close to me
That holocaust such rhymes depict
Spread fiery tongues of flame which licked
At my own family.

THE SPIRIT

Should EIGHTY FOUR DAYS serve no other useful purpose, its compiling brought about the reunion, thirty years after the Battle, of the Reverend Canon W. D. O'Hanlon and Squadron Leader Geoffrey Wellum, DFC. This memorable occasion had for its setting the ancient church of St. Nicholas, Studland, Dorset, where the Canon is now resident. No words can describe the impact of privilege upon the bystander at such a meeting. Truly my feet trod hallowed ground that day.

--- * ---
*

THE PILOTS' PADRE

The Chaplain at Biggin Hill Station was Padre and
    friend to the 'Few'.
'Twixt offering alms and oblation he flew with the
    comrades he knew.
A fugitive priest flying ferry, winged men on short-
    leave thro' the sky.
His subterfuge quite necessary, for rules forbade
    Chaplains to fly.

Yet, he was a qualified pilot, possessed with great
    knowledge of flight:
A soldier of Christ among airmen who diced in that
    grim game with Death in the height.
I met him full thirty years after, compassion etched
    deeply in brow
Which neither his jokes or his laughter succeed to
    disguise, even now.

The names of young pilots, wolves tore from his flock,
    quick-phrased in the flash of recall
As pain dulls his eyes with the echo of shock deeply-
    wrought at the news of their fall.
I watched him yarn-swopping with one of the 'Few',
    'old-comrade' to him, and my friend.
Then spellbound in privilege gained a mind's view
    of how that great Battle made end
To tyranny, slavery, and Evil's sword, for both wore
    the armour of Right.
The Canon who wielded the Power of God's Word
And the pilot whose Spitfire was Christ's in the fight.

German and British airmen alike crashed to their doom into the Channel. Others flopped crippled aircraft onto its heaving surface. Yet more baled out of uncontrollable or blazing planes; many with their flesh terribly burned and hanging in grotesque blisters. Others were critically wounded. Even those unscathed by Battle or fire were subjected to severe shock and exposure. And no more despairing plight could be imagined than that of a man forced to abandon all contact with humanity to bob helplessly as a tiny speck on a watery waste. In daylight, apprehension of rescue would be acute. But with gathering darkness hope faded for many for ever. Nevertheless, many men of both sides were plucked from such plight and owe their lives to the vigilance of searching aircraft and rescue launches of the Royal Air Force Air Sea Rescue Branch and the superb German Seenotflugkommando.

*
*

THE QUALITY OF MERCY

Throughout the long embittered fight
The stricken men of either side
By parachute from blazing plight;
By useless engine's luckless glide;
Were cast from heat of Battle hell
Into a cold and lonely swell.

THE QUALITY OF MERCY

The Channel claimed a thousand men;
Their fates unknown; their graves no mark;
Exhausted souls succumbing when
A spark of life fled hopeless-dark.
The cruel sea respected neither side
And keeps the secrets locked beneath its tide.

All men are one when they must fight the sea
And to the luckless airmen succour came
As friend and foe fought common enemy
To rescue all in mercy's hallowed name.
May history applaud with equal pride
The air-sea rescue teams of either side.

Though I speak with the tongues of men and of angels, and have not charity, I am become as sounding brass, or a tinkling cymbal.

St. Paul
1 Corinthians, chapter 13

———————— * ————————
*

FIRST CORINTHIANS THIRTEEN

They ain't sure 'e's a Jerry, mate
So don't you cheer too soon!
The Copper finks 'e's one of our'n
Wot 'it our own balloon.
But judgin' be the bits wot's left,
Then Gawd abuv can tell.
I only see 'im comin' down
Like blinders out've 'ell.
Pore Bugger, mate, 'oo'ever 'e might be.
I don't wish that on no one, no, not me!

If that was yore boy down that 'ole
I don't fink you'd be glad.
Orlright, if 'e's a Jerry, then,
Ter me it's bleedin' sad.
I don't serspose 'e wanted war
No more than you nor me.
One fing's fer sure, e's 'uman, mate,
Don't care wot side 'e be.
The Vicar's prayin' fer 'im jist the same.
Let's dig 'im out, so's 'e can say 'is name.

Any Battle of Britain aerodrome was a veritable hive of industry. The technical complexities of the then modern fighters demanded a thousand skills. Engine and air-frame fitters, riggers, armourers, radio technicians, ground-handling crews, transport drivers, petrol bowser drivers, photography experts, doctors and nurses, storekeepers, building maintenance workers, administrative personnel, typists, and of course, those involved in aerodrome defence.

A special word for the magnificent work of the Controllers and their Staffs who literally steered the pilots into the Battle. However, almost without exception, the controlling brains were located away from the aerodromes.

Essentially, everyone had to be fed, so along with the mundanity of everyday domestic requirement, the catering staffs, the batmen, and all those who served performing quiet daily tasks, deserve recognition.

All suffered attack and men and women from all branches were wounded and killed.

It would be fitting to remember here also the miraculous tasks performed by civilian post office engineers who worked long hours through great dangers repairing and maintaining the vital telecommunications of Fighter Command throughout the Battle.

---------- * ----------
*

THE FORGOTTEN LEGION

A word for the unmentioned legion - the bods that
   supported the 'Few';
Their gruelling hours of laboured sweat helped the
   Hurricanes fight in the blue.
To refuel and rearm a Spitfire meant muscle and toil
   every day,
For each plane demanded attention and some needed
   parts shot away.
They slept where they dropped thro' the Battle; their
   waking hours spent at the task
Essential to aircraft and pilot, they gave more than
   any dare ask.
Mechanics refurbished tired engines; the riggers
   patched up shattered wings;
A swarming host of other types lent a hand to a thousand
   odd things.
An army of girls drove the bowsers and worked in a
   motley of trades
From parachute-routine-inspection to squinting at
   radar screen 'fades'.
They pressed-on despite daily bombing, and bearing
   the brunt of attack,
Were wounded or killed by the hundred, but courage
   was never in lack.
Behind the great and gallant 'Few' those men and women
   fought
And by their blood and sweat and skill the victory was
   wrought.

Any chain is as strong as its weakest link. The dynamic punch that Fighter Command packed in 1940 literally derived its strength from a unique chain of co-ordinated equipment, machines and personnel.

The Chain Home Radar Network formed the prime vital link giving advance warning of enemy air activity across the Channel. Secondly came a duofold combination of the Royal Observer Corps, supplementing with locally observed information the radar scans already tracking the enemy. Such information was then fed into the Filter Rooms of Fighter Command Headquarters at Bentley Priory. From there it was transmitted to the Groups, and thence forwarded in terms of direct command to the Fighter Stations. Each station reacted immediately by dispatching pilots, who then depended on Ground Controllers to feed them with up to the minute information right into the battle zone.

The broadcast instructions to pilots were, of course, equally available for enemy interception and the unique code jargon used by the 'Few' was a vital contribution to the ultimate efficiency of such a close-knit system.

That having been said, no volume seeking to perpetuate the memory of those momentous days of the Battle of Britain would be complete without a portrayal of the radio chatter and banter crackling through battle-tormented ether in the summer of 1940.

SCRAMBLE! is an almost literal adaptation of passages occurring in REACH FOR THE SKY, the biography of Group Captain Douglas Bader by Paul Brickhill.

——————— * ———————
*

SCRAMBLE!

"Two-Forty-Two Squadron scramble! - Angels
  one-five to North Weald."
As 'phone-bidden pilots race yelling, twelve
  Hurricanes thrum on the field.
Then, spinning wheels tucking in flap-trailing
  wings the pack thunders into the air,
"Laycock Red Leader to Steersman! Am air-
  borne and on our way there."

Bader's formation of four vics astern climbs
  steeply to South thro' the haze,
His painful eyes probing the high starboard sun
  concealing attack from their gaze.
"Hallo Laycock Red Leader! Steersman receiving
  you clear.
Vector one-nine-zero. Buster!" commands the
  cool voice in his ear.

"Sixty-plus bandits approaching North Weald."
  the Duxford Controller relates;
Then Merlins are screaming at full boosted revs
  as throttles are slammed thro' their gates.
Nine thousand feet and still climbing with rev-
  counters running amok.
"Blue Leader to Laycock Red Leader! Six aircraft below - three o'clock!"

SCRAMBLE!

Over the rim of his cockpit Bader sees dots well
    to beam,
"Blue Section investigate!" he clips - in the
    moment he spots the main stream.
Three Hurricanes peel-off to starboard and
    vanish into the opaque,
"Bandits at ten o'clock level!   Wait 'til I tell you
    to break!"

The dots become a swarm of bees in glinting rows
    revealed;
Their steadily droning North-East course is
    headed towards North Weald.
Bombers in tidy lines of four and flying six
    abreast
With Messerschmitts above, below - still more
    above the rest.

They'd have to risk the fighters and go for the
    Dornier swarm.
"Green Section!   Take the top lot!"   His voice
    is cool and calm.
Green Leader zooms his vic of three away and
    up to right;
Three more of Bader's Hurricanes committed to
    the fight.

"Red and Yellow Sections!   Line astern with
   me! "
Six Hurricanes go screaming down guns blazing
   vengefully.
Black crosses!   Glinting perspex!   Swim thro'
   illumined sights;
Thumbs triggering squirts of tracered hails that
   score in splashing lights.

Suddenly the drilled lines burst in mad turns right
   and left;
A running ripple splits the ranks the Hurricanes
   have cleft.
Among the melee scattered herd the gallant six
   lunge on;
A Messerschmitt's belly in Bader's sights
   explodes and then is gone.

Oily blossoms, smoking trails - a torrent of
   belching death;
In perspex capsules many die or gasp their
   anguished breath.
Bader's blood is racing now, his nerve and muscle
   taut;
Careering madly thro' the rage his Hurricanes
   have wrought.

SCRAMBLE!

Slowly curling in stalled-turn a Messerschmitt above!
He reefs his nose up after it and triggers with his glove.
One hundred yards and closing fast - a full three seconds squirt;
The Messerschmitt rocks fore and aft then seems to hang inert.

Flame bursts along its starboard wing - both engines are ablaze;
A tiny figure tumbles from the glinting perspex glaze.
And then it spins in fiery doom towards the fields below,
Where distant plumes of rising smoke the pyres of victory show.

Exhilaration from the kill is chilled at fleeting glance -
The mirror just above his eyes betrays by Fortune's chance
His victim's comrade slanting in with tracer-flicking guns -
And in the heat of battle Bader roundly curses Huns!

SCRAMBLE!

Steep-turning hard and spiralling he thwarts
   avenging foe
Who vanishes beneath his wings in steepish dive
   below.
He dives to chase it streaking East like some
   bat out of hell
Behind the scattered bomber force now fleeing
   home pell-mell.

Dry mouthed, sweating, breathing hard - as tho'
   he'd run a race,
It startles him to realise the height he's lost in
   chase.
So pulling up he steeply climbs returning to the
   fight;
But in the sky that was so full no aircraft are in
   sight!

"Phenomenal this empty sky which brims with
   battle's rage
Then seconds later empties like some new turned-
   over page!"
He scans the victory pyres below with pride and
   joy - but then -
A sudden stab of sobering thought - some might
   be his own men!

SCRAMBLE!

"Laycock Red Leader to Steersman! We gave
'em a bloody fine chase!"
"Steersman to Laycock Red Leader. Good show!
You can pancake at base."
A gaggle of Hurricanes circles the field and
Bader's joy bursts in a grin;
"Eleven!" he notes with a surge of relief and him-
self is the last trundling in.

As pilots return from dispersals the Station
Commander's face masks
The strain of his long anxious moments, "Did you
get among 'em?" he asks.
They piece all their stories together with facts
of the battle revealed -
Not one single bullet in twelve Hurricanes - nor
a solitary bomb on North Weald.

Doubtless many domestic pets were highly useful in their ability to hear the ominous warnings long before their human masters. Such advanced notice was invaluable, as it enabled Mum to shepherd the kids to the shelter, grab the cakes and lemonade, and then give her that vital extra time in which to go back for the insurance policies!

--------- * ---------
*

OUR EARLY WARNING SYSTEM

"The cat's gone on the shelter, Mum, the sirens will
   soon go."
And sure enough the sirens' sound soon rent
The summer air with wailing pitch alternate high
   and low -
The Luftwaffe was winging over Kent.

The wailing ceased, the sirens moaned then murmured
   in the heat;
A pregnant prelude calm before the raid;
Then first the distant engine-hum took on that well-
   known beat
Of Dorniers and Heinkels on parade.

OUR EARLY WARNING SYSTEM

Crescendo-roar above your head was sound to re-
assure -
The friendly-busy sound the Merlins made;
The Brylcreem Boys were climbing up - each man to
fight a score;
By radar vectored to their place of "trade".

The throbbing heavens filled with din and wispy vapour-
trails
As eight-gun fighters hosed their cross-marked prey;
And men and metal showered down midst tracer-
streaming hails
While people wondered, "How many today?"

The "all-clear" went, the lace-trails swelled to
dissipate in space;
That glorious September mocked its slain,
"The cat's gone on the shelter, Mum, he's heard the
sirens go."
And thus the show repeated yet again.

The incident depicted is factual. An afternoon raid became a dogfight shambles over the roofs of North London homes. The aircraft, a Messerschmitt 110, literally flew along the street with pilot and gunner plainly visible. Tracer bullets streamed from the gunner's weapon into the Hurricane no more than twenty-five yards on his tail. The Messerschmitt was obviously doomed when flame licked from its port engine and our group of schoolboys cheered and danced with glee. Admonished by my Mother, we no doubt felt that she was "square", but retrospectively it is realised that she was representative of all mothers and that the following verse might well be dedicated to the Unknown Warrior.

——————— * ———————
*

TO MY MOTHER

The sirens smote the afternoon with banshee knell
of death;
The high winds quilted heaven with the feathered
bomber-breath,
And so we stood and watched them as they vaulted
England's gate;
A thousand engines bellowing their Nazi hymn of
hate.

TO MY MOTHER

But suddenly the quilt was slashed by criss-crossed
   vapour-swords
As Spitfires reached the zenith of the swarming
   German hordes,
The quilt became a tangle as the massed formation
   broke;
Discordant engines drowned the hymn as vapour gouted
   smoke.

Then stricken bombers tumbled down emitting tortured
   wails;
A dozen dived to roof-top height with Spitfires on their
   tails;
One Messerschmitt flew down our street - the gunner
   fought like mad;
The Hurricane hard on his heels blazed everything he
   had.

An engine spewing gobs of oil, that gunner still fought
   on;
A gout of flame as he flew past denoted he was
   done.
Oh! How we cheered that Hurricane which sped with
   vengeful guns,
But Mother said, "You mustn't cheer - poor men -
   they're someone's sons."

Pilot Officer Percy Prune was a cartoon character well-known amongst the 'Few' and the entire RAF. Prune used to illustrate what pilots should not do. In other words, if Prune did it, you didn't!

———————— * ————————
*

PRUNE FLIES AGAIN

Oh!   To be back in the office
Among the knobs and things.
To scream off down the runway,
And rise on gleaming wings.
Whanging thro' the ether -
Like the Mercury bloke in the myths
Then a glance at the fuel gauge,
Blimey! Nothing showing - 'cept SMITHS.

That football pitch below me
Looks long and smooth and green.
I head the old-girl for it -
The touch-down's fast but clean.
The players quickly scatter -
But one bloke does a flop,
The port-wing hits his noggin hard
Then brakes full on, we stop.

PRUNE FLIES AGAIN

I'm petrified in the cockpit -
The prop is in the net!
Strewth! That was ruddy close, old lad!
You always did forget!
I think of the poor bloke I clobbered,
The terror I've just brought about.
They'll know I forgot the fuel-gauge!
Arthur Mitchell is bound to find out.

Then a cheering crowd rushes towards me,
They're shouting for all they are worth -
Not paying the slightest attention -
To the poor injured bloke on the turf.
The running mob reaches the aircraft,
They give me a wave and they shout.
So pulling myself together
I slide back the hood and climb out.

Then a pompous old gent is shaking my hand,
As speechless, I stupidly stare
At the golden chain around his neck,
The old boy must be the Town-Mayor!
"Sharples is my name, sir -
I'm Mayor of Sidley Town,
Which will never forget the wonderful way -
You lobbed this aeroplane down!"

"By Gad! You're a wonderful pilot -
And a jolly keen sportsman, I see!
But how you spotted from right up there
That the game was off-side, sir, beats me!!
With swift and precision-like judgement,
Of the highest and noblest degree
You steered thro' twenty-two players,
And clobbered that crooked referee!"

The summer of 1940 was an era full of tensions and emotions. No one, without experiencing first-hand the frustrations of being attacked whilst utterly defenceless, could understand the seemingly unlikely motives of the hero depicted. But as a boy who frequently fired a Diana air pistol at low-flying Nazi planes, I can state that any attempt to strike back, however futile, is more fruitful to the relief of tensions than to remain passively terrorized.

By and large, those most affected by the Luftwaffe's assault and its ensuing nightly Blitz were the poorer classes of London, particularly the East End. And if asked to name one quality which enabled these folk to withstand the threat of flaming destruction; violent death or worse; daily and nightly, then I would name that quality without hesitation - Cockney humour. If there was one not too secret weapon which defeated the Nazi dream, this was it. The true Londoner, among whom I am proud to be numbered, has a built-in capacity to withstand the most frightful assaults on his way of life, or indeed, life itself, and yet still see the funny side of a situation.

*
*

ONE OF THE FEW

So there was jist me an' this Junkers - an' I only 'ad
  me ole bike;
Cor! It drove me near stark starin' bonkers for fear
  I should die, sudden-like;
Oh! 'Twas orlright for them wiv their Spitfires - they
  'ad lots o' poke to 'it back;
But orl I 'ad got was me bike-pump - an' a few pound
  o' spuds in me sack.
I was bikin' 'ome from me allotment - a pint at the ole
  Bee'ive first;
Wen I 'ears this 'ere sudden explosion - an' I finks that
  me innertube's burst.

Anuvver one went as I freewheeled an' as I looked up
  in the sky,
I sees this 'ere flippin' Looftwaffer wiv cotton-wool
  puffs driftin' by;
'Is crosses was plainer than tombstones an' there 'e
  was comin' at me;
I finks about chuckin' me taters - corse that's orl I
  'ad, d'yer see?
I'm sure if I 'ad I'd 'ave 'it 'im, but wot I'd 'ave done
  I don't know.
'Is injines seemed 'orribly 'ealthy an' my pore ole bike
  was so slow.

ONE OF THE FEW

I jumps orf an' grabs up an 'ouse-brick. Then jist as
    'e buzzes me 'ead
I 'urls it wiv orl I can muster - an' one of 'is injines
    stops dead!
Jist then there's a rattle of bullets - a Spitfire dives
    right on 'is tail -
Ole Jerry 'e wobbles a couple o' times an' kicks up a
    terrible wail.
That cheeky young cuss in 'is Spitfire was 'avin' a go
    at my 'Un -
I 'spose 'e decided that 'e'd be orlright wen 'e see
    wot me 'ouse-brick 'ad done.

That Looftwaffer flops like a jelly an' bang goes me
    ole 'lotment shed;
But then this young bloke wiv the Spitfire does 'is
    vict'ry-roll over me 'ead!
'E opens 'is winder an' gives me a wave, "You clear
    orf!" I shouts, proper mad.
"Don't you try pinchin' my glory, ole mate - that's the
    very first Jerry I've 'ad!"
Well, I don't serpose 'e could've 'eard me, but anyway
    orf 'e soon flew;
An' I writes an' tells dear ole Winston - count me an'
    me bike wiv yore 'Few'.

Told in the parlance of the day, all events depicted were factual. Though failing to couch well-pronounced adjectives in suitably flowery phrases, the average Londoner's version of objective reporting is without equal.

——————— * ———————
*

ONE OF THE MANY

Them Looftwaffers came over 'undreds strong, an'
   ev'ry day we saw our Spitfires fight;
I seen 'em 'ave a proper ole ding-dong - them vapour-
   trails was quite a pretty sight;
Now an' then you'd see one comin' down - their 'igh-
   pitched wails kicked up a proper racket;
A vapour-trail would turn a dirty-brown, an' one of
   Gorin's blokes 'ad copped a packet.
Cor, Mate!   We 'ad one at the back of us -
A Messerschmitt - the bloke got fried, pore cuss.

The day they plastered Croydon, I recall, we watched
   'em goin' over big an' black;
An' as they went we see a dozen fall - they nearly
   scraped our chimney comin' back;
Our 'Urricanes was pottin' 'em like flies - a ruddy
   Messerschmitt flew down our street!
Our bloke stuck to 'im 'opin' 'e would rise - but we
   could see as 'ow 'e was cold-meat.
That gunner fought as we watched 'im descend -
'E 'it the sewage farm at Ponders End.

ONE OF THE MANY

Anuvver time we see 'em bomb Norf Weeld - they tried
  ter git our fellers on the ground;
An' 'Urricanes wot used some uvver field got stuck
  into 'em like a pack of 'ound -
We saw some Jerry parashoots that day - a Dornier
  came down near Southbury Road;
A Stuka copped it somewhere Epping way an' blew ter
  smivvereens wiv orl 'is load.
Yerse! I remember them September days -
Them boys of ours performed beyond all praise.

Corse, then ole 'Itler couldn't keep it up - 'is Looft-
  waffers was beaten fair an' square;
'E found as 'ow 'e 'ad been sold a pup - an' 'im an'
  Gorin' fell out then an' there;
'E chewed 'is carpet then 'ad umpteen fits while Gorin'
  tried 'is very best persuasion
Ter be allowed ter start 'is London Blitz - at night 'is
  Looftwaffers might find occasion
Ter sneak an' drop their bombs wivout a fight
An' make up fer 'is losses in the light.

So ev'ry night 'is flippin' bombers came - an' let me
  tell yer that it was no joke;
But ev'rybody carried on the same amongst the broken
  glass, the dust an' smoke.
They set the docks along the Thames on fire an' once
  the flippin' City was alight;
You 'elped ter keep yer neighbours out the mire an'
  London burnin' was a sorry sight.
But cheer an' courage reigned in ev'ry street -
Yer see - we knew our pilots 'ad 'im beat!

My two sisters and I were blessed during the dark days of 1940 with a Mother of great patience and fortitude and a Father who was a veteran of the First World War's ghastly struggle. For many years we had listened to Dad's stories of the trenches but no matter how he humoured them they still gave us a glimpse of the horrific reality of war. Apprehensive though we were, when that great testing time came, he took it all coolly in his stride and his attitudes are portrayed factually in the following rhyme.

*
*

THE OLD SOLDIER

Blimey!   What a man he was, that veteran of
    Passchendaele;
Emphasizing obscene threats with thumb stabs in
    the air;
Strolling up the garden path, impervious to
    shrapnel-hail,
Encouraging the Spitfires that were mixing it up
    there.
"Shoot the blanking blanketies and put the fear of
    Christ up 'em!"
(Indeed, he was a master of the British Soldier's
    Tongue!)
And in the rain of jagged steel from shells the
    gunners flung at them
You'd hear him singing parodies his Army pals
    had sung.....

THE OLD SOLDIER

> Oh, oh, oh, it's a luvly War!
> What would'ye do with eggs and ham
> When you've got plum and apple jam?
> Oh, oh, what d'ye say
> Ain't it a shame to take the pay?
> Oh, oh, oh, it's a luvly War!

Strewth! Was he a cool one? That old warrior
    from Neuve Chapelle -
(Royal Corps of Signals with the Fighting First
    Northants).
Years before he'd fought 'em in that bloody trench
    and barbed-wire hell,
When any Prussian fretting him stood precious
    little chance.
"Don't you keep on ducking, lad - when I say
    "duck!" - you bleedin' duck!"
(The British Soldier's epithets that echo down the
    years).
When at night the screeching bombs would bid you
    scamper terror-struck,
He'd chant another ditty with a glee that vanquished
    fears.....

> Sammy! Send up a flare.
> Sammy! Right in the air.
> Now over there you'll see a German
>   sniper.
> Pass the word along to Captain Piper.
> Sammy! Send up a flare.

Lucky? Christ! I'll say I was, to have him there
   when times were grim;
He made you feel invincible thro' Britain's darkest
   days.
Skilled in war so long before with courage oozing
   out of him;
Dispelling apprehension with his humoured turn
   of phrase.
One afternoon the bombers came, and grabbing
   me he shouted, "Duck! "
I found myself beneath the hedge with him on top
   of me.
And there we sprawled in safety only yards from
   where the missile struck
With my dear Dad, the soldier, serenading
   cheerfully.....

     When this wicked war is over,
     Oh, how happy I shall be!
     When I get my civvy clothes on
     No more soldiering for me.
     No more going home on short leave,
     No more asking for a pass;
     We will tell the sergeant-major
     To stick his passes up his ......!

1940 was a year of bewilderment to the children and teenagers trying to make sense of all that was happening about them. Parents, relatives, neighbours, donned uniforms; some to remain living at home; some to disappear from the vicinity; some never to return. The call for volunteers both from the Forces and the civil organizations was constant and loud and those of us in our teens were able to perform at least some slight task which identified us with the great War Effort.

———————— *
————————
*

A BOY AT WAR

Sad girls in gym-slips and crepe de Chine blouses;
Shy boys in jerseys and grey flannel trousers;
Cardboard-boxed gas-masks and tag-label strings;
Porters and teachers who planned journeyings
To Highlands of Scotland, or Canada-far;
To Monmouth, Tredegar or Leamington Spa,
This how I remember our school refugees
Who then I much envied as 'evacuees'.

They later related adventures abroad;
Of living in homes few could ever afford;
Of life in the country with horses and cattle,
Remote from the dangers and din of the Battle
That we who remained had observed every day -
Had even been part of, we proudly could say!
So thanks to my parents in London I stayed,
A messenger boy in our grand Fire Brigade.

A BOY AT WAR

Proud of my uniform, tin-hat and mask;
Proud of the men who commanded my task.
No men did more in the Battle than they
When Dowding's 'boys' made it so costly by day
That Heinkels and Dorniers slunk in at night
And fire-storms became a new battle to fight.
So men of 'B' Station across from 'Ridgeway'
Your boy now salutes you in this later day.

For nostalgic chats and instructional talks,
On Coventry Climax and Beresford Storks
Which you used in battles of holocaust fire
(Then made me take cover or bade me retire!)
'Knock-on!' and 'Knock-off!' were your strange
  battle cries
As death and destruction rained down from the skies
So stoutly defended each day by the 'Few'
Compelled as night fell to hand over to you.

But this is much more than a tale of small part
And privilege of one who was 'in at the start',
For I was a boy and a million like me
Then did what they could to some tiny degree,
Whilst too young to fight yet acutely aware
Of all that would follow defeat in the air.
This merely my view to which hosts could add more
Of how Britain's kids were affected by War.

Late in the Thirties the Air League of the British Empire saw the need to foster a spirit of air-mindedness among Britain's youth. Towards this end the Air Defence Cadet Corps was created along similar lines to those of the Boy Scout movement. But as the War muddled through its early stages, the Air Ministry translated the Cadet Corps into the Air Training Corps - though at this stage such recognition was hardly more than token. The new Corps mushroomed into a great company of youngsters, veterans and skilled men motivated by an enthusiasm which gave patriotism purpose as well as feeling.

———— * ————
*

VENTURE ADVENTURE

The Air Defence Cadet Corps' name
Was not long-lived but just the same
It was foundation-stone for fame
Earned by the ATC.

Air Training Corps absorbed young ranks
Which owed the Air League debt of thanks
For birth when battleships and tanks
Held high priority.

Officialdom discouraged boys
From interest in "costly toys"
When cavalry or gun-boat ploys
Were Empire weaponry.

Sad-late they saw the awful truth
As proud fanatic Hitler Youth
Forsook frail glider like milk tooth -
Luftwaffe fang to be.

Thus British lads were spared the horse
To learn of flight and signal Morse,
To navigate a foreign course
By other means than sea.

So while the 'Few' held Freedom's Gate
In schools and church halls - somewhat late
Trained flying crews decreed by Fate
To flatten Germany.

Stout veterans helped turn that tide
Till those they taught exemplified
A fostered hope then justified
By amateurs, maybe - but very skilfully
And Democratically!

From the Luftwaffe's point of view, the Battle of Britain was intended as a softening-up prelude for Hitler's "Sealion" plan to invade Britain. The vital stroke was to knock the fighters of the Royal Air Force out of the sky in order that the seaborne army could cross the Channel with certain air supremacy. Of course, the Luftwaffe failed and the invasion threat dissolved in the smoke of crippled Heinkels and Messerschmitts limping to their bases in the closing stages of the Fight of the Few.

But the threat remained a very formidable possibility during the Battle and many measures were taken to harass or hinder the German parachutists who were expected as the advanced guard of Hitler's invading forces. One such measure was the removal or painting-out of all road signs.

——————— * ———————
*

FOUL WORK AT THE CROSSROADS

We've put up wiv ole 'Itler droppin' bombs an'
  flippin' mines;
An' Looftwaffers a'playin' merry 'ell.
But now they've gone an' painted out yer ruddy
  crossroad signs,
Jist where you are's impossible ter tell.
An' Gorin's blokes still finds their way about
Wivout no signs nor pilots lookin' out!

It beats me where these bowler 'ats gets all
  their bright ideas.
Ter fool the Jerries?   Blimey wot a stroke!
It's us wot's lorst an' if the German Army soon
  appears
Ter try an' find 'em won't arf be a joke.
"Go at once ter so an' so," they'll say.
"Righto!" says our General, "But wot way?"

In 1940, aircraft recognition had become an essential art which has survived as a hobby similar to the pastime of train-spotting. Silhouettes of friendly and enemy aircraft were displayed in the National Press and in public places. Hundreds of detailed books on the subject of aircraft recognition were also on sale. The true masters of the art were the men of the Observer Corps whose task was vitally linked to Fighter Command's defence network. Long since the Battle this essential organization has rightfully earned the prefix 'Royal' and today's enthusiasts are welcome in their ranks.

---- ＊ ----
＊

AIRCRAFT RECOGNITION

In days when Britain's skies posed lethal threats,
Her population studied silhouettes
Of Goering's air force types, then daily banes
And umpteen different shapes of our own planes.
The egg-shaped tails of Heinkels and a one-o-
    nine's square wing,
Twin rudders on the Dorniers and Junkers' forward
    sling
Of engines lined with noses, much like Blenheims
    otherwise,
Or the diamond tail of Ansons, then so common in
    our skies.

And what about old Lizzie, our Lysander's fond
  nickname?
The Proctors and the Magisters with Moths of
  Tiger fame?
Whitleys, Hampdens, Wellingtons, so very common
  then?
The evil crook-winged Stuka and the Messerschmitt
  one-ten?
Somehow we got to know them and to spot them in
  the air -
We even learned the sounds they made then had no
  need to stare.
Our Hurricanes and Spitfires were the easiest to
  tell,
Their Merlins droned a throaty tune which cast a
  calming spell
Above the threatened fields or streets where pilots
  fought attack,
The Spitfire with its pointed wings; the Hurricane's
  hump-back.
Until we learned in later day quick way to tell them
  all -
The Nazis only flew one way - then wailed in
  plummet-fall.

Another anti-invasion measure was the forbidding of church bells being rung except as the signal for impending arrival of invading forces. The night of Saturday, 7th September, was one of intense German air activity and a comparatively junior officer issued the codeword "Cromwell" to all the Southern Defence Chiefs. Men hurriedly left their homes to man road-blocks and prepared positions in order to fight off the long-expected vanguard of parachutists. They did not know that the order had been issued in the absence of a Senior Commander and their apprehensions are not difficult to imagine. Many places in the South of England heard the dreaded church bells, and Potters Bar, on the outskirts of London, was among that number.

Thankfully it was a false alarm, but the rumour-mongers had many field days. Thousands of dead German soldiers were floating in the Channel; there had been a terrific battle at Worthing; the Navy had set the sea alight at so-and-so and hundreds of invading Germans had perished horribly. In fact, not one solitary German soldier set sail that night nor any other night. But before the error was realised some bridges were actually blown at the behest of the "Cromwell bells".

————— * —————
*

CROMWELL'S CLANGER

Church bells ringing loud and clear.
Good God! The German hordes are here!
And Cromwell's peal bodes little cheer
Against the bombers' drone.

"I say, Major! Is that right?
There _are_ a lot of planes tonight.
Inform Brigade and just sit tight -
I'll have to use the 'phone."

"Captain, muster your platoon.
Brigade will issue orders soon,
And when the moment's opportune
Make sure your bridge is blown."

"Strewth, Liz! What a blinkin' night!
There's us all scared and set ter fight;
Then daylight comes - sod all in sight!
A bloomer by some clown!"

The term 'number eight' was a household word throughout the days of the black-out.   It seemed that the torches available then were designed for this type of battery.   All too often they were in short supply and had to be queued for, like many other commodities. People laughed and made jokes about the black-out as they took it, like most other wartime inconveniences, in their stride.   But thousands of people were killed and injured in accidents directly attributable to the enforced and necessary total darkness.

———————— * ————————
*

THE SMALL TORCH OF FREEDOM

The weapon of most in the black-out was a battery
   called 'number eight';
At a time when they cried, "Put that light out!" without one you'd be in a state.
Identity card and a gas-mask were carried thro'
   bomb, shot or shell;
And when you went out in the evening you needed a
   flashlight as well.
Oh! They did what they could about seeing by painting
   all sorts of things white;
Like all bumper-bars and the mudguards of cars but
   you stumbled and sprawled in the night.
They had a good wheeze when they painted the trees, the
   lamp-posts and things in the street.
Tho' unprintable verbs over tripping-up kerbs followed
   adjectives equally sweet.
An air-raid at night was a heart-pounding sight and you
   wondered if your turn was next;
But a welcome searchlight helped diminish your fright
   as it banished the darkness which vexed.

That was all long ago and we won, as you know, thro'
   the grim days which Churchill termed 'great';
So whilst voicing our due to the great gallant 'Few',
   here's a small one to our 'number eight'.

Although pots and pans made of aluminium were nothing near so commonplace as today, the housewives of 1940 made loyal response to the appeal for such metal articles to be melted down and used in aircraft construction. Piles of assorted objects grew from village greens and beside Air Raid Wardens' Posts in the towns. The majority of these contributions were in the form of saucepans, kettles, flasks and camping or cycling accessories.

*
*

ALUMINIUM

Your saucepan could cook-up a Spitfire;
Your kettle put 'T' in its name;
Your 'dixie' be part of the best fire
And camp in this grim battle-game.
So housewives forsake the utensils
Which melted could help build a plane,
And let them fly high 'neath the stencils
Of Freedom on some Hurricane.

Recorded fact with no further comment required
or given.

———————— * ————————
*

THE LAW IS AN ASS

There's this bloke finds a bomb in 'is ceilin'.
'E gits it down onto 'is back,
An' while flippin' London is reelin'
From Looftwaffer bombs an' attack,
'E chucks it down in this bomb crater
Where soon it goes orf wiv no 'arm,
'Til up comes a copper jist later
An' nicks 'im wivout any qualm!

Now if you serpose I am ribbin' -
I swear on me oaf it's a fact!
This Majistrate gives 'im a wiggin',
An' under the Hexplosiffs Act
'E goes on and finds 'im one 'undred crisp
    quid!
I arsks yer, mate, 'ow would you feel?
Instead of a medal fer 'avin' got rid,
They found 'im five quid on appeal!

Perhaps the first 'sweater-girls', the women's Land Army grappled with the vital task of replacing men on the land. Girls, who weeks previously had been afraid of mice, were driving tractors, milking cows, and mucking-out pigsties. All this at a time when "Dig for Victory" was the slogan of the day. Though mundane, their contribution was paramount, for the Nation still had to eat.

———————— *

* ————————

LAND GIRL

Joan was the girl who got wed to my chum, a
   tar in the Navy was he.
While totting-up days with his 'sippers' of rum
   he entrusted his lover to me.
"Look after her while I'm away. I'm counting
   on you, mate."
And that is how, first-hand, I'll say, Land
   Army girls were great.

Now if that makes you snigger, then you've
   read my meaning wrong,
For loyalty - especially then - was something
   pure and strong.
These priceless girls forsook their homes to
   fight upon the land
And what they did was what I learned in terms,
   as said, first-hand.

They scorned their scents and powder-puffs
to toil in muck and mire.
The cow-shed and the pigsty hardly went with
sweet desire.
Boots and breeches, jungle-hat; in shirt and
tie they dressed -
But oh, those tight green jerseys silhouetting
youthful breasts!

Our Town girls ploughed good British soil.
They tilled and sowed the land.
Soft hands, rough-calloused by such toil, did
all that Man could stand,
And many stretched their aching backs in
Essex fields or Kent's
To watch those massive air attacks meet
Spitfires in defence.

When many German airmen made their first
ignoble walks
To the local village bobby at the threat of
land-girls' forks!
But back to Joan. She married Frank and
raised three gorgeous kids
And represents tough, lovely girls who laugh
at burn-bra libs!

No claim is made to any record of six men attempting to take on a Nazi invading force. But in the early days of its formation, indeed, in the immediate aftermath of Dunkirk, when England's need was most dire, the Local Defence Volunteers, later to become the Home Guard, were in fact pitifully equipped as depicted and a working musket would have been a luxury weapon. Retrospectively, such endearing terms as DAD'S ARMY come easily to mind but it was no joke at the time!

Forming the backbone of the LDVs were the combat veterans of the First World War trenches, and although outclassed in terms of weapons and equipment, the force would at least have given the Germans a terrific headache had their invasion dreams materialized.

DAD'S ARMY

Our HQ had just had a 'phone-call and tensed at the
   message received;
The Germans were dropping their parachute-troops
   in the manner we'd always believed;
The Captain gulped down his pint-Guinness and ordered
   a large tot of rum;
For weeks he had drilled us in what we should do and
   now our big moment had come.

He called all his men to headquarters - and that
    caused a hullabaloo,
For he issued his order at one-forty-five and the
    Crosskeys chucked-out after two.
His men soon reported for duty - not one of their
    number did fail,
And bravely they heard their instructions whilst
    swigging down pints of brown ale.

Bob Jenkins, the old village postman, had 'phoned in
    to give the alarm;
He said that he'd just had a close-one by the duck-pond
    near Hollow-tree Farm.
There must be well-nigh on a thousand, and one nearly
    got him, he said;
The German had uttered some terrible cries as he
    floated down over Bob's head.

So six men, five pikes, and a musket, marched boldly
    to meet with the foe;
But what they would do when they met him was some-
    thing they didn't quite know.
Approaching the Hollow-tree duck-pond they crawled
    in the ditch by the road;
Expecting to hear shots each moment and see German
    troops by the load.

Nearer they crawled to the duck-pond - with never a
    Nazi in sight;
They then saw a parachute hanging, snagged high on a
    tree, limp and white;
It billowed in soft-silken ripples whenever the slightest
    breeze moved;
The German troops were there all right - as the
    dangling parachute proved!

No doubt they had buried the others, and now they lay
    hid in the wood;
Six Englishmen facing a thousand were odds you could
    hardly call good.
The Captain looked long at his wristwatch - he couldn't
    think what else to do;
He knew he should try to outflank them - but that would
    be hard with so few.

Then right in the midst of dilemma, a man came and
    looked in the ditch;
He spoke in a strange foreign accent, but the Captain
    could hardly tell which.
"Please tell me where I find ze 'phone-box - I have to
    bale-out of my plane -
If I get ze word to my squadron - they come and they
    fetch me again."

The Captain could tell he was German for he was a
   hard man to trick;
"Look-out, chaps!" he yelled to his soldiers, "They'll
   come with a rush in a tick!"
The 'German' stared hard at Bob Jenkins - "I see this
   man here and I shout -
'Don't run please, you must stay and help me', but
   then I fall hard and pass-out."

"My Spitfire is crashed in ze wood somewhere - please
   help me to look for ze wreck -
I clobbered two Nazis before they get me - I'm an
   RAF pilot - I'm Czech."
The Captain looked hard at Bob Jenkins, "A thousand
   at least did you say?
You only saw him and stopped counting - and he saw
   you running away!"

They all went to look for the Spitfire and found what
   was left in the trees,
But only one parachute saw they that day and it dangled
   and swayed in the breeze.
Of course, they were not disappointed and things had
   worked out for the best,
But poor old Bob Jenkins is talked of today - and it's
   years since they laid him to rest.

During research interviews it is surprising how many old warriors can be prompted into amusing recollections merely by mention of the name of some well-known household product. Both 'ERE! - 'AVE A WOODBINE and PASS THE MARMALADE are typical examples.

———— * ————
*

'ERE! - 'AVE A WOODBINE

We smoked 'em in the trenches 'mongst the 'orrid oozy
   stenches an' in shell-'ole isolation up at bloody
   Pashondale -
As we marched the Menin Road, flippin' 'undreds of
   'em glowed - but we cupped 'em in our 'ands, like,
   to avoid a bullet-'ail.
When the Kaiser called "Enough!" - we was relishin'
   a puff in a shy retirin' dug-out up at 'Wipers'
Where we 'eld our celebrations - givin' 'eed to
   'esitations brought about by unrelentin' Jerry
   snipers.
Fifty years an' more we crossed the Rhine -
An' then as now I smoked me old Woodbine.

'Course, then came 'ole 'Itler's War - 'twas "The
   mixture as before", and I found me self fire-watchin'
   in the Blitz;
An' just like in the lines, as we dragged at our
   Woodbines, we cupped 'em in our 'ands because of
   Fritz.
Fings blew-up an' fings came down, and our "front"
   was London Town but uvverwise fings 'adn't changed
   a bit;
We ducked the muck an' flame, an' we carried on the
   same - an' smoked our Woodbines in the thick of it.
I'll soon be joinin' them old pals o' mine -
An' 'ow could 'eaven lack me old Woodbine?

Dedicated to many of the old age pensioners of the 1940 era who accepted the dangers and trials of the period with equal fortitude and humour.

———————— * ————————
*

PASS THE MARMALADE

What a story he told - he was ninety years old - of his
    exploits in three bloody wars.
He was clipped on the Somme, dodged a Luftwaffe bomb
    and was captured by Smuts' ragged Boers!
At our breakfast table, he laughed at the label that
    girded the marmalade jar;
And spellbound we listened, while two bright eyes
    glistened with mem'ries he drew from afar.
When he saw "Hartley's" on the marmalade
His mind flashed back to Kitchener's Brigade.

"We was in the Transvaal, an' meself an' a pal made
    a charge wiv the Yeomanry Force;
But it got out of 'and 'cos the Boers made a stand, an'
    we bofe got run down by an 'orse!
Well, we couldn't get back - we'd outrun the attack -
    an' our bruises was 'urtin' us sore.
As we crawled to escape, some big bloke wiv a cape,
    said that we was 'is pris'ners of war.
An' from their loot of Kitchener's Brigade
We watched 'im spoonin' 'Artley's Marmalade!

116

Nineteen 'undred an' one - as the New Year begun -
   I was only a bit of a kid;
But it came back so clear, as I sat wiv you 'ere -
   when I saw "'Artley's" name on the lid.
Then the Kaiser's War came, an' the same flippin'
   name was a luxury up on the Somme;
Wiv Maconochie stew you 'ad 'Artley's jam too - an'
   fer afters Fritz chucked you a bomb!
I don't know now, 'ow old that firm must be -
But any'ow, they're least as old as me!

When ole 'Itler's War came, it was no bloomin' game -
   'cos they shoved all yer jams on the rashun.
I was sixty yer see - so they didn't need me - an' ter
   queue at the shops was the fashion.
Well, I'm standin' in line, when the ole sireens whine,
   so I summons me soldier's aplomb;
Then we 'ears engines 'um - an' them Looftwaffers
   come - an' me 'ouse blows sky 'igh wiv a bomb!
An' that's why I'm alive ter make me boast -
I'd better shove this "'Artley's" on me toast! "

What can induce nostalgia or stimulate memories better than some long-discarded popular refrain?

World War 11 saw the miracle of radio, adapted in its many complex forms and used for good or ill. The very pilots fighting in the skies depended upon it to a great extent for their ultimate success. All the combatant powers used it for propaganda. Radio provided a potential quickly seized upon by Goebbels' Propaganda Ministry, while here at Home, the British Broadcasting Corporation contributed immeasurably to the Nation's morale in its darkest hour. If anyone doubts the high morale of our Nation during the threat of Nazi invasion and throughout its prelude of aerial assault, they have only to listen to some of the songs we sang or play back some of the hilarious ITMA radio programmes portraying the humour of the beloved Tommy Handley.

The British Broadcasting Corporation was also engaged in "War Work". At the time of the Battle and later it provided vital code-links with the underground partisans still opposing the Nazis in Occupied France.

The total war effort was a demanding business for all the men and women of our Nation. But any man, soldier or civilian, asked to name the woman of the hour, would answer "Vera Lynn", for the songs she sang were legion, and "There'll Always Be An England" became the Nation's Battle Hymn.

THE SONGS WE SANG is intended as a salute to all the artistes who boosted our morale and entertained us when we needed them most.

———— * ————
*

THE SONGS WE SANG

In ode to the stumbling black-out my most vivid mem'ry
    recalls:
The words of the prophet composer who wrote WHEN
    THE DEEP PURPLE FALLS;
A host of those wonderful medleys in Charlie Kunz'
    soft-pedal style,
THERE'LL COME ANOTHER DAY he played - it did,
    and now we smile;
That still surviving evergreen with Turkish rhythm
    touch,
We sang and danced to Cole's BEGUINE and tones of
    dear old "Hutch";
WE'RE OFF TO SEE THE WIZARD so Judy Garland
    sang - it knitted very nicely with the flier's "Wizard
    Prang!"
The song of kids in shelters throughout that summer
    fine -
WE'RE GONNA HANG THE WASHING ON THE
    SIEGFRIED LINE;
Flanagan and Allen's songs became the Nation's habit,
Airmen, soldiers, kids alike were chanting their
    'RUN RABBIT';

THE SONGS WE SANG

WHO DO YOU THINK YOU ARE KIDDING MR.HITLER?
  chided Flanagan when times were grim;
LORDS OF THE AIR sang Gracie Fields - the Battle's
  timely hymn -
THERE'LL ALWAYS BE AN ENGLAND - and so we
  had to win!
The Forces Sweetheart (still enthroned) was lovely
  Vera Lynn -
Her English voice so crystal clear brought sunshine
  thro' the rain.
And I expect that Johnny has his little room again!
Al Bowlly's golden voice was stilled when Cafe de
  Paris
Was blasted in the London Blitz - here's to his memory!
And who remembers in those days of battles in the air,
Enchanted evenings - even then - that echoed with
  MY PRAYER ?
SOUTH OF THE BORDER DOWN MEXICO WAY was
  just the ideal place to dodge the bombers every day!
Despite the bombing from the air A NIGHTINGALE
  SANG IN BERKELEY SQUARE -
And for what I know it could still be there!
Thro' "Dangerous Moonlight" and bomb-blasted days
THE WARSAW CONCERTO won well-deserved praise;
WHEN THE LIGHTS GO ON AGAIN ALL OVER THE
  WORLD
Wistfully sung as the black-out blinds rolled;
LONDON PRIDE MEANS OUR OWN DEAR TOWN TO
  US -
LONDON PRIDE IS A FLOWER THAT'S FREE - Thus
The late Noel Coward wrote during those dark days -
It was then - It still is - Thank God!

Field Marshal Rommel, upon being informed of the assault on the Normandy beachheads (June 6th 1944), told his German colleagues that that day would be the Longest Day. If that were true, it could have stood no comparison with the Battle of Britain described by Churchill as the Finest Hour. Rommel felt that the fate of Nazi Europe would be decided in the first twenty-four hours of the Allied invasion. In fact, the fate of Nazi Germany had been etched in the skies of Britain nearly four years previously.

——————— * ———————
*

THE LONGEST HOUR

They came like swarming locusts in the blue September
    haze;
Their engines filled the sky with throbbing din;
The dissipating vapour-trails would drift and then
    erase -
To be replaced by others swarming in.
A thousand silent sentinels contrived to keep them
    high;
Balloon Command performed its task unsung.
The firemen waited ready and the ARP stood-by -
Watching crumps of scything-steel the gunners flung.
The kids sang in the shelters as the bombs and bullets
    sped,
Defiantly they sang, 'Run, rabbit, run!'
And cheered the roaring fighters that went speeding
    overhead
To intercept and decimate the Hun.
"Their finest hour" were Churchill's words of praise;
A longish hour - it lasted eighty days!

RED DUSTER

Avast!   Make-fast, secure to glories past
An epic line from Britain's greatest fight,
As a third-mate's running log
Records slaughter, sea and slog,
Aboard merchantmen which passed in Battle's
    night.

When they steamed from sight of shore,
Lay beyond the "phoney war",
For the sea took heavy toll from very start,
Many ships fell early prey
To the battleship "Graf Spee",
'Til the Royal Navy ripped her plates apart.

Off the beach from doomed Dunkirk
Seamen died at Mercy's work
In a hell which shattered armoured fighting
    ships.
Not forgetting stalwarts staunch,
Manning paddle-boat or launch,
Who were blown to bits while making rescue-
    trips.

Then first shots in Britain's Battle
Came with Messerschmitts' death rattle,
While the Stukas aimed their dives at convoy
    steamers.
So, as they attacked our ships,
Chain Home Radar saw first blips,
And the "phoney war" at last deserted
    dreamers.

Hungry wolves in U-boat packs
Mounted merciless attacks,
In the West Approaches many sailors died
On a stenching-slick alight
By torpedoes in the night
Guts and lungs choked-up with oil in freezing
    tide.

Petrol needed by the 'Few'
Came at price which greater grew,
And the cheques were drawn in Merchant Navy
    lives.
Men who died in Freedom's Name
In a thunderbolt of flame
Or in ocean depths where no account
    survives.

Massive convoys setting sail
As a foreign sun grew pale
Were impressive fleets of two-score ships and
    ten,
Which by next or second dawn
Had been scattered wide and shorn
With a loss of half the vessels and their men.

But the crews who braved the foam
Prayed with all the folk at home
That Britannia's Sons would triumph in the
    air.
Every tanker they brought thro'
Meant full-tanks among the 'Few',
While each cargo staved starvation's bleak
    despair.

They continued without falter
When defeat seemed fate of Malta,
And once more the need was fuel for fighter-
  plane.
At incredible a price just one tanker's short
  suffice
Tipped the scales of narrow margin yet again.
Our Merchant Navy's proud traditions then
Are focussed in 'Ohio' and her men.

THE MEMORY

London's East Enders were called upon to make unspeakable sacrifice as the Luftwaffe's prime target after Goering switched his tactics to bombing their city. Tactics which virtually saved the precious airfields upon which the 'Few's' operational survival depended. Consequently, there is a unique relationship of participation between the Londoners and their priceless 'Few'. Compelled to observe and share in the effects of the Battle from 'ringside seats', the most authentic comment is to be found in their tongue - which has yet to be seen publicly engraved. But during that time the walls of bombed out buildings could be seen bearing inscriptions in chalk which emblazoned Cockney defiance throughout the heat and hate of the Battle - "London can take it!" - and it did!

*
*

TO THEIR MEMORY

To the mem'ry of our airmen
Poets much more great than me
Wrote in words of educashun
Tributes fine fer folks ter see.
Words abart the sun's new-dawnin',
Magner Carter, Runnymeed;
Words us Cockneys wot was born in
London's East End orften read,
But fer simple reason we don't write
'Cos that ain't 'ow we fink.
An' Cockney treason owns no right,
So I shan't try ter wink
At our down ter earf plain langwidge
Used in Smiffield or the Docks.
Slang wot ain't exactly Cambridge
Spoke by mates in council blocks.

Wen it comes ter plain brass tacks, mate,
Tho' we don't talk BBC,
We got sense enuff ter preshyate
Wot our Air Forse did. Stone me!
Walkin' round our East End markets,
Stepney Green or down the Lane,
Posh words fit ter go on carskets
Won't be 'eard - jist talk wot's plain.
As yore rubbin' Cockney shoulders,
Anywun wiv eyes ter see,
Grasps the fellership wot smoulders
London Town's fraternitee.
Ev'ry 'eart's a flippin' gold-brick, mate,
An' none gives tinker's cuss
If yore 'ome's in Bow or Reigate,
While yore there yore wun of us.

Named amongst our fallen airmen
Many lads wot spoke our tongue.
Boys from night-schools wot was carmen
Climbin' up anuvver rung.
Lads from butcher's shops an' fact'ries,
Tally-clerks from London's docks.
Busmen tort ter fly on Sundays
After miles of stampin' clocks.
We fond remember orl our boys -
An' them from betta class.
Speshly them on that September
Wot we watched wen broken glass
Was the floor of London's Dockland
An' got deeper wiv each clout
Burstin' while we cleared the muck, and
Learnt wot war was orl about!

127

So tho' sentiments are diff'rent
None are more 'eart-felt than ours.
We don't talk abart magnifsent -
That's fer posher prosy flowers.
But we slogged the Blitz wiv orl our boys
Froo fire an' bomb-blast 'ell,
While we dug our cots an' kiddies' toys
From mounds wiv gruesome smell.
"'Andsome!" mate, that's wot we'd say,
One Cockney word ter say it orl.
Which should be Magner Carter way
On Runnymeed's memoriorl.
"To orl of them, from orl of us,
While Cockney sparrer's wings may buzz.
Our deepest fanks wiv little fuss,
Fer 'andsome is as 'andsome does."

"Beyond our reach in London's sky
Them Boein's an' our Tridents ply,
                    Born free.
On wings of peace each speedin' trace
Paints mem'ries in gold-wispered lace
                    Fil'gree.
'Cos wen we see them vapours first
All 'ell the City's skyline burst.
                    Yer see,
'Twas first ole Gorin's planes wot wrote
Same sky-write score, but diff'rent note,
                    Wiv glee,
Wen sireens wailed instead of jets,
Which wunce 'eard then, no mind fergets,
                    An' we
Remember as that Jumbo plies
Where Spitfires swatted 'Itler's flies
                    Daily,
Each VC. 10's majestic noise
'Ymns debt still owed to Dowding's Boys
                    An' 'E,
Wot saved this England wiv 'is brains,
'Is Spitfires an' 'is 'Urricanes,
                    Like flea
An' dragonfly compare
The side of TriStars in the air.

The world fergets, but as it larfs,
More planes keep scrawlin' epitaphs
                  . Which flee
To drape bright shrines beyond our sight
Of those who fell in Freedom's fight.
                    Eternally. "

Radar was as vital a weapon to the pilots of the 'Few' as were their Spitfires and Hurricanes. The names of Robert Watson-Watt, Henry Tizard and Hugh Dowding are those of an immortal trio whose untiring efforts produced the technology which did so much to baffle and thwart Goering and his cocksure intentions.

_____ * _____
*

TRIUMPHANT TRIO

Inventor, Robert Watson-Watt, was held in great amaze,
For "killer-watt" - so rumour said - had harnessed
    deathly rays.
In secret quest he wryly smiled and laboured with
    resolve
Thro' daunting times of fail and test to prove his
    Klystron valve.
So as the gathered clouds of Europe grew
He forged the "magic-weapon" of the 'Few'.

Scientist, Henry Tizard, gave co-ordinating mind
And skill of two test-pilot hands for proving things
    designed
To aid our fighting airmen gain the mastery of skies.
With pioneer grit he ground the edge of Dowding's
    "big surprise".
Then, Radio Location was its name
Eventually as Radar to win fame.

Veteran, Marshal Dowding, nursed the baby right from
    birth.
From early days at Biggin Hill he seized upon its worth.
So when they made him Fighter Chief the Battle's fate
    was sealed,
For he was dour Professor of the weapons he could
    wield.
Invisibly, the scabbard of his Sword
Was woven by the wings of Goering's horde.

In contrast with the sunlight dogfight battles, the ominous drone of night raiders could strike terror into the hearts of all but the very brave. The "night shift" was almost the sole province of the anti-aircraft gun and searchlight batteries. And the sight of a raider, relentlessly pinned in the concentrated spotlight of a dozen searchlights, wretchedly attempting to dodge the maelstrom of sprinkled deadly beauty, was awe-inspiring.

It could hardly be said that the magnificent men and women manning these units went quietly about their task!

——————— *
              * ———————

SEARCHLIGHTS AND SHRAPNEL

A hostile bomber droning somewhere in the night.
Reverberating window panes and glinting dewy tiles.
Sinister foreboding, clandestine flight,
Cloaked in the cloud-cloistered heavens it defiles.
Incandescent blinding shimmering stabs illume
Horizon's darkened rim, suffused with milky-glow,
Grows silhouettes - the London skyline loom
Hardening with each new brilliant probing throw
Until inverted fans of roving fingers ringing
The menaced city, floodlit now, displayed
At risk to vibrant hidden villain winging;
Yet confident that he soon be betrayed
Above beloved Capital cluster, as by day alert.

Ah! A tiny moth! A fleeting darting glimpse in sweeping
   beam;
The dazzling fingers move as one, and there, inert,
The fugitive! Swimming in spotlight pool like a silver
   fish agleam.
Concussions! The raucous crash and thunder of
   artillery;
Echoes rumbling, grumbling, fading; a pausing pregnant
   calm.
Aloft! Myriads of jewel-flash pyrotechnics. Trajectory
Punctuated paragraph of war. Explosive sequinned
   storm
Of gouting jagged steel and scattered death.
Crumps! Remote cordite cacophony whoofs at earth.
Concussions! Muzzles bark and flash with flame-
   crack breath.
A faltering, the jewelled fish tumbling, a dearth
Of pity for stricken raider spinning down the height.
Dipping now to torture shattered victim to the last
A criss-cross trellising of angled light.
Impact! Disintegrating bomber's orange splash and
   blast.
The fingers probing pitilessly in radiant lust for more;
All goes quiet, one by one the arc-fed shafts retracting;
The mantled dark oppressive as before
Seems thicker now. A distant bomber's drone . . . . .
 . . . . a re-enacting . . . .

Air history's dead have their own very special place in our consciences but what I have asked our poet to depict is the origin of a situation which somehow implanted in me a permanent and quite unaccountable guilt complex. It is in fact rather more than that; it is a reminder of the way in which the mutilated and the mentally scarred, thrown on the scrap heap of World War 11, are today too easily rejected and forgotten.

I can only hope that the sincerity and delicacy of Barry Winchester's interpretation will succeed in transmitting to others this same sense of obligation that will for ever be owed to these men.

6.11.73   GEOFFREY AUSTIN CHAMBERLAIN
                              ARAeS, AMIIE

A BLENHEIM'S GUNNER

Midnight and such a commotion;
A summons tattoo'd on a pane;
The shouts of a neighbour in anguish;
A turmoil of thoughts thro' my brain.

Adrenalin boosting my action;
A handspring makes short of the fence;
My torch brings astonished reaction
To mute yet traumatic events.

He lies on the stone in his nightmare;
Pyjamas half-drape his burned trunk;
Gloves still concealing lost fingers;
His right ear a mis-shapen hunk.

Pathetic and silly his wig knocked
    askance
Shows garish by light of the torch
Now miniature spotlight by long-after
    chance
On war's grim and vicious debauch.

I ponder the window ten feet o'er my
    head,
Amazed he's unharmed from the jump,
Still screaming the warnings he yelled
    as he sped
In Blenheim, to dead pilot's slump.

"Skipper! That Messerschmitt hit me!
I can't stand the flames - we're on fire!
We'll have to bale-out - give the order!
For Christ's sake! It's melting the
    wire!"

He still screams distraught as the
    ambulance leaves
In nightmare the years bring again
To brand on my conscience a night which
    bequeathes
Stark grasp of that Battle's remain.

Holiday-makers and visitors to the seaside resorts of the Isle of Thanet have, over the years, made the short detour via Manston Aerodrome where a Spitfire has stood for all to see. Although of somewhat later vintage than the Spitfires actually used in the Battle, it is a true representative of its honoured breed.

It is astonishing that nobody saw fit to preserve for posterity more specimens from Britain's most decisive struggle. Nevertheless, the devastating attacks on Manston Aerodrome during the Battle; the airfield's proximity to the French Coast, and the open aspect of the Kentish countryside, somehow permeate the pilgrim's mind with nostalgia when he clambers about this neat and lone Spitfire with its flaking paint and weathering fabric.

THE LONE SPITFIRE AT MANSTON

Do you still remember them - that gathering
Of eagles fighting in a summer sky?
Spitfires, Hurricanes, diving, zooming, hovering,
Crescendo engine-roar for battle cry?

How can we weigh the measure of the years -
Forgetfulness whereby frustration springs?
Aggressive courage earned them fickle cheers -
The echoes fade - like paint on tarnished wings.

136

Men of the Works Department, at the end of the year, are replacing the Windsock at the shattered north end of Biggin Hill Airfield. A few yards away are the remains of the Bomb Shelter where forty WAAF were killed. The old windsock is on the ground at the foot of the mast.

SONNET TO A WINDSOCK

Dedicated to Tommy Lund and his friends of 92 Squadron

Brave canvas by a thousand breezes worn!
Now on some dirty scrap heap to be thrown?
These rents are wounds of war by Germans torn -
A hundred hard-strained eyes on thee alone
Depended to be guided into land
After the fight.
Eyes of my friends and now
Some are no more.   All these, waiting with hand
On stick and throttle, glanced at thee, made vow
To give a good account and in that glance
Looked last on England, climbed up into cloud
And flew away for ever.
John fell in France
And Bill in flames,
For Peter sea was shroud.
Shall danger-money* workmen end thy year?
"Leave it with us!" Their voice is in our ear!

DECEMBER 1940   DOUGLAS O'HANLON
                               Chaplain (C of E) RAFVR

* Civilians with danger-money earned more than most
  of the pilots who flew over them.

137

The Battle of Britain brought new dimensions to the fascinating hobby of Aeromodelling, for up to that time model aircraft were the mysterious pastimes of a stalwart few. But when the Government saw the need to foster a spirit of air-mindedness among the youth of the day, from which it had to draw the pilots and aircrews for a rapidly expanding Royal Air Force, Britain's model industry was truly born. As well as interest, the hobby provided an excellent means of learning the then all-important art of aircraft recognition. Soon, soldiers on remote gun-sites, sailors at sea, airmen on airfields, men of the Observer Corps, firemen, policemen, etc., all were busily acquiring the "balsa-butcher's" art. But the stocks of imported balsa wood soon seemed exhausted and substitute light woods, such as the obeche, began to be used. To the "solid-scale" modeller this even had advantages and presented no real tragedy, but to the flying-model fraternity the lack of balsa posed a serious challenge.

Today's middle-aged enthusiasts now relish those days with nostalgia steeped in momentous history. Names like Skyleada, Skyrova, Studiette, Slick, Astral, Truscale, Joy-Plane, Airyda, Skybirds, and CMA were all household words at that time. Frog, of course, were already pioneering today's plastic scale-solids in the form of then unique and beautiful miniatures.

But outstanding in meteoric rise to fame was the name Keil-Kraft. Eddie Keil, along with his local designer, Albert Hatfull, produced a range of flying-scale and duration models which were simply superb. Spitfire, Hurricane, Lysander, Messerschmitt 109, Defiant, etc., introduced a flying-scale range contemporary with the duration models, 'Ajax' and 'Achilles' which commemorate to this day the victory of their namesakes over the Atlantic pocket-battleship raider, Graf Spee. Moreover, all the range was of high quality and in balsa wood, capable of greatly excelling the modest claims of Eddie Keil. No words here could express more than the statement that this same range has been included in the vastly expanded catalogue of Keil-Kraft throughout all years since. The first Ajax built by the author achieved OOS* on its maiden flight. ROG* from an Enfield recreation ground at four o'clock one afternoon, it was fished from the Thames at Woolwich at 7.30 p.m. Happily it survived and after retrieval logged many long flights.

Eddie Keil was born into the furniture industry where he acquired the skills of operating wood-working machinery later put to use in supplying cut balsa to the trade. A keen modeller, he competed internationally and was flying petrol-driven models in the Thirties.

A familiar figure on Hackney Marshes, but particularly Fairlop, Eddie had time for all enthusiasts, young or old, expert or novice. Some years ago he moved his premises from Hackney to the impressive modern factory at Wickford, in Essex, which now conducts the largest business of its type in Britain.

*OOS - out of sight   ROG - rise off ground

On November 13th 1968, the aeromodelling trade mourned its founder while thousands of enthusiasts suffered the loss of a great pioneer who had given inestimable pleasure and instruction to untold millions.

The role Eddie played throughout the War years was far more important than might today be realised, but it is not forgotten by those who had the privilege of knowing him.

—————— * ——————
*

PIONEER PATRIOT

To Eddie Keil of Keil-Kraft Model fame, a timely
    mention of the things he did.
A tribute to beloved Cockney frame in shirt and braces,
    crowned with trilby lid,
Which in the model world swelled Cockney pride,
The champion, our counsellor and guide.

The Battle's challenge captured youthful minds, of we
    who watched and daily cheered the 'Few',
So reminiscence relishes reminds of Eddie's kits we
    proudly built and flew:
Spitfires, Messerschmitts and Hurricanes
From tissue, balsa wood and rubber skeins.

But where that balsa came from is a mystery to this day
    in the model trade, whose Founder never told.
To Patriot of patriots it came straightforward way for
    his 'brook-no-nonsense' honesty was bold.
And somehow, Eddie, right throughout the War
Maintained supply of balsa kits galore.

Synonymous with Keil-Kraft is the 'Graf Spee' battle's
    fame and in any model aircraft shop today
Present youth buys pioneer fliers on which Eddie built
    a name, for his 'Ajax' and 'Achilles' are for aye.
When Britain craved air-minded youth, then rare,
In Eddie Keil came answer to her prayer.

Contrasting sharply with the silvery splendour of
the barrage balloons were the drab squarish gasbags
carried atop many vehicles. Petrol was a precious
commodity, won at high cost of Merchant Navy lives
and tonnage. A simple conversion allowed petrol
engines to run on gas but the obvious disadvantage
was the bulky gasbag often as large as the vehicle itself.
Some forms of transport towed a small anthracite
burner unit in order to produce gas on demand, and
such oddities today would raise many eyebrows in
expressions of disbelief.

———————— * ————————
*

GASBAGS

Balloons in the air;
Balloons everywhere;
Some amongst stars;
Others on cars.
High facing enemy;
Low bringing grocery;
Hydrogen filled for flight;
Car-bags of anthracite.
Oh, what a boring sight!
Captive balloons!

Thousands of tin hats serve out their exile as hanging ornamental flower baskets. The accompanying is an ode to one in particular.

———— ✳ ————
✳

ME OLE TIN LID

Wire-baskets slung from tripod chains
Grace porches thatched wiv creeper-trains,
But not in ours - I used me brains,
I 'ung me ole tin-'at!

Terday it 'angs there upside down,
Jeraniums an' moss in crown,
While ivy creeps from rusty brown
Which orften starts a chat.

I was a warden once, d'ye see,
An' that there ole tin-'at an' me
Can tell a tale or two - p'raps three
Of shrapnel's zip an' splat.

ME OLE TIN LID

I even wore it in me barf -
Go - on! I know, they always larf!
But when ole Jerry used ter strafe
'E pounced jist like a cat.

I sometimes 'ung it by me bed -
More often up all night instead -
The Missus larfed one night an' said,
"We makin' luv with that! ?"

Oh, yerse, she always liked 'er joke
An' froo those days of fire an' smoke
I knew I was a lucky bloke
To 'ave a wife like Pat.

But she changed when the War was done,
She said, "Orlright, you've 'ad yore fun.
No Germans now, nor bomb nor gun,
Throw out that tit-fer-tat!"

She pinched me buckets an' me torch,
Me stirrup-pump which once damped scorch,
An' now me lid 'angs in our porch -
She moans it rusts 'er mat.

But that ole 'at's me coat of arms
An' best of all me lucky-charms -
Froo bombin' 'ell an' false alarms
I wore me ole tin-'at!

So when admirin' them there flowers
Jist give a thought fer umpteen hours
It kept me dome from shrapnel showers
Of zip an' plop an' splat -
An' ping on that there 'at!

As far as the children and schoolboys were concerned, 1940 saw the demise of many of their favourite characters as the War took toll of their weekly entertainment. BUTTERFLY, JESTER, JINGLES, PENNY WONDER, SUNBEAM, TIGER TIM'S WEEKLY, TINY TOTS, TIP TOP, and TRIUMPH were compelled to cease publication and hundreds of well-beloved characters were finally laid to rest. For the schoolboys and teenagers of 1940, perhaps the greatest tragedy lay in the extinction of Frank Richards' Greyfriars and all the lovable pupils of that famous establishment. No doubt the mention of many weeklies will bring a nostalgic response to those middle-aged today, but surely none more than mention of the MAGNET.

——————— * ———————
*

146

THE GHOSTS OF GREYFRIARS

"Yarooooooh! Oh crumbs! Oh crikey!"
  groaned Bunter in his day.
"Just serves you right, old fat man!"
  Bob Cherry used to say.
"The rightfulness is terrific!"
  (Hurree Jamset Ram Singh).
"Why you fat, footling, frabjous fraud!"
  was Wharton's rendering.
"Boot the ass!" growled Skinner. "Oh,
  my hat!" gasped Johnny Bull.
"Kick him!" threatened Vernon-Smith,
  "Let Coker eat him whole!"
"Postal-order come at last?"
  smiled Lord Mauleverer.
"Oh, really, Mauly!" Bunter cried, "It's
  mine - I mean - I er....."
"Cave! Quelch is coming!" Bolsover
  major warned.
"Oh, let him catch the fat chump!"
  Frank Nugent harshly scorned.
And so they'd vanish down the stairs
  while Bunter clutched his feasts.
"I say, you fellows!" yelled the Owl,
  "Don't leave a chap - you beasts!"
The Bounder tried to save the thief
  but Quelch was not denied.
"Upon my word, you wretched boy!
  What cause have you to hide?"

THE GHOSTS OF GREYFRIARS

So once again the game was up and
    Bunter's bags were beaten.
He weekly drank a bitter cup for
    stolen tuck he'd eaten.
But still we loved him dearly and
    fond memory aspires
To glad pre-Nineteen-Forty days
    before they blitzed Greyfriars.

In an age of forgotten values and inane abuses of hard-won Freedom, "Go to it!" would seem to be meaningless. But in 1940, whatever Freedom's price, it was a price that had to be paid. Our Nation has long forsaken a sense of common purpose to drink deep of a placebo labelled "What's in it for me?"

* * *

GO TO IT!

Today is the dark day of treason, disguised by an abuse
  of 'free',
When greed has dispelled common reason and nothing
  else matters but 'Me'.
We once were a patriot nation with but a small handful
  of spivs
And everyone manned their own station in War which
  this volume relives.

The people were one in grim effort, to win or to die
  was their choice.
Surrender was nobody's purport as Winston gave tongue
  to their voice.
The old and the young swelled the factory; our women
  toiled long with their men;
With only the best satisfactory; when quantities rose
  beyond ken.

GO TO IT!

The struggle gave birth to a kinship; the challenge
   won Freedom today,
But spivs still make killings from hardship -
   'Developer' sounds more au fait -
And so we have words more high-sounding for subtlety's
   sake when at peace,
But those who usurp Freedom's founding, drink
   warrior's blood from quick-lease.

Those who love self before others are those who are
   virtually dead;
Sick vampires who suck widowed mothers whose kin
   for our country have bled.
So let us remember in straightforward terms words
   like 'treason' and dark 'treachery',
Think less about football and pool-coupon perms to
   contemplate skulduggery.

Freedom is not just a carve-up for some but something
   equality owns.
It's no right to strike for a blackmailer's sum nor the
   sanction of slogans and moans.
The Nation got by on just three little words which
   wrought us a miracle then;
"Go to it!" was not ancient chaff for the birds, it is
   sanity's call to forsake the insane.

The men of the Luftwaffe were, for the greater part, humble men drawn from ordinary homes. No useful purpose would be served by an examination of the shortcomings of Nazi leaders who dictated the fates of so many in the Battle. Though difficult to separate the warrior from his cause, the fact remains that the young men of Germany performed their fearsome duty with great courage.

"Who art thou that judgest another man's servant?" Romans 14 : 4

———————— * ————————
. *

TO THE LUFTWAFFE

How shall we remember them? The Messerschmitts;
Those cross-marked Heinkels, Dorniers and Junkers?
Messengers of death in Goering's terror-Blitz
We watched from threatened streets or garden bunkers.
Sequin clusters throbbing in the summit
Of summer's sunlit vapour-tangled sky,
Disdaining comrades doomed in stricken plummet
Or chimney-hopping too hard hit to fly?

TO THE LUFTWAFFE

What then shall we say of him? The enemy
Who sought to lay us low at any cost;
A word at least, completing this epitome
Of how we won the fight he fought and lost.
A worthy foe who fought for noble cause?
Alas, such epithets deny disgrace
On Führer-heiling national applause
Of heinous rape upon the human race.

What then can we say of them?   The flying crew
That daily smote our land in frightful fashion.
To kinfolk mourning German sons and fathers who
In English graves were laid with all compassion.
Unto our fellow men who fought let this
Short line be spared in our commemoration,
Courageously, in duty led amiss,
They fought and died with honour, for their nation.

At the eleventh hour of the eleventh day in the eleventh month of the year 1918, an Armistice terminated the awesome carnage wrought by the greatest war of all time. Rightfully recorded as the Great War, the gruesome toll of human lives represented the most horrific human tragedy of all history. When the War, that had become bogged down in the Flanders mud, the battlefields of the Somme and the bloody impasse at Verdun, stagnated into trench warfare, a seemingly harmless invention, bestowed upon humanity by the needs of the cattle-ranching West, gave dreaded words to the parlance of both the German and British Armies. Barbed wire! In a waterlogged, muddy hell, the luckless soldiers of the opposing armies daily performed great deeds of fruitless valour. Millions of living men were transformed into grisly corpses as they struggled to penetrate the flesh-rending obstructions in the face of decimating rifle and machine-gun fire.

Above that holocaust flew cloth and wood flimsy aircraft of the newly-formed Royal Flying Corps. And the contribution of this new arm of the fighting forces towards the conduct of that far-off War was magnificent. But the truly decisive role of our airmen was yet to come.

In 1918 the Royal Flying Corps became the Royal Air Force, the baby of the Services. Who could foresee that Britain's naval and military might would one day become impotent, as was our Navy in 1940, and defeated, as was the Army's Expeditionary Force in France? Fortunately, there were men who with remarkable foresight strove to equip the new Royal Air Force for such a contingency. Outstanding amongst these men of vision was Air Chief Marshal Dowding who encouraged the development of the radar and air-control radio systems which tipped the scales in the Battle of Britain. 1940 saw Britain alone and almost defenceless against the Nazi war machine which had by that time extended its fighting front to the beaches of Normandy and Cap Gris Nez. Foremost amongst the Nazi triumphant forces was its mighty and victorious Luftwaffe. Poised for the final assault against the British homeland, the German fighters and bombers prepared to scythe a path for their invading armies. To achieve this the Luftwaffe had only to destroy the comparatively small force of Fighter Command. This having been accomplished, the way would have been clear for invasion. The life of Britain was at stake. But also, as was later recognized, so was the freedom of all mankind. The outcome of the ensuing Battle of Britain is recorded in history. And although it may be truthfully said that the soldiers, sailors and airmen of the two world wars laid down their very lives for freedom, no battle was more vital or significant than was the Battle won by Churchill's precious 'Few'.

For many years we have perpetuated as a day of mourning for our war dead, the eleventh hour of the eleventh day in the eleventh month of every year - and rightly so.

However, the gallant 'Few' have a commemorative week in every September. During this week of the 'Wings Appeal', the Nation honours Churchill's 'Few'. It is a week reserved for a tiny force of men whose deeds of valour outstandingly set them apart in the Nation's history.

---------- * ----------
*

TO YOUTH

How could you visualize?   A gathering
Of eagles fighting in the summer skies,
A tumult rage of aeroplanes; diving, zooming,
    hovering,
Tormented engines screaming battle cries.
How could we know the terror and the thrill?
Sheer desperation forcing them to dare;
Their lives dependent on a thread of skill,
They fought those bloody battles in the air.
How could we grasp the horror and the hate
That brimmed the heart that watched its
    brothers smitten,
Or understand the torments of a fate
That vividly relives a page long written.
How to describe the streams of tracered steel
That sought to pulp young flesh in youth's sweet
    bloom,
Or yet perceive the wounds that none can heal,
Shock-wrought by sight of friends in blazing doom.
How can we justify their fateful years
If apathy be all the fruit they bear?
Aggressive courage earned them fickle cheers
From many who have long since ceased to care.
What long delirious days they were!
Steeped deep in fear - disguised with banterings.
What anguished thoughts of sacrifice they stir,
The tumble-glint of sun on shattered wings.
Lest we forget; be mindful of their place,
For Freedom's price was pain and blood and
    sorrow.
Tho' young in heart they bore their years with
    grace
And gave their yesterday for our tomorrow.

THE ANOMALY

Perhaps the greatest affront to the 'Few' and the dead heroes of their small company was the wining and dining at the Royal Air Force Club, Piccadilly, in October 1973, of Hitler's Armaments' Minister, Albert Speer - by indiscretion of media men.

Speer, one of the younger members of the Nazi party, was primarily an architect. Hitler's marble halls and his palace of grandeur, the Reich Chancellery, were among Speer's creations. He was not only the architect of the Nuremberg Stadium (intended by Hitler as the "World's" Olympic Stadium after his conquest of the globe!) but also the architect of those fantastic Nazi mass rallies.

Nuremberg had other portents for Speer and the Nazi thugs when it provided Freedom's Judgement Seat before which Speer went into confinement for twenty years.

At this time, the farcical anomaly of Speer's freedom and Hess' eternal incarceration continues.

--- * ---
*

VAMPIRE'S VISIT

Doenitz' U-boats, Belsen's wire,
Delights of my decree.
Yet Nuremberg's all-cleansing fire
Left hardly singe on me.
I made the Führer's tools of Hell;
Sieg-heiled at every rally;
Made Goering's bats, his bombs as well,
(We three were very pally).
Death came to many Nazi pals
By choice or neck-rope sever
But Speer may come and Speer may go
While Hess is chained for ever.

THE EFFECT

OF THE ABANDONED FINALE

There is no margin for doubt as to the importance of Fighter Command's victory. Had they lost, the British Navy, deprived of air cover, would have been hard put to prevent the German Army invading and occupying Britain. Hundreds of reconnaissance photographs, taken by Royal Air Force reconnaissance aircraft, provided massive proof of the German invasion fleet congregating in readiness for the assault. Hitler's abortive operation "Sealion" cost the German taxpayer many millions of marks. With typical Teutonic thoroughness, a highly detailed programme had already been prepared for the administration of conquered Britain. And Hitler's infamous henchman, Reinhard Heydrich, had already appointed Britain's SS Overlords. Armed with Himmler's Sonderfahndungs-liste (Great Britain), the occupying Nazis would have rounded up thousands of prominent people named for the Gestapo's attention. Exactly what might have happened had the 'Few' succumbed, can only now be a matter of speculation. For the first time the occupying German Army would have been harassed by partisan forces using arms and equipment stored for that contingency <u>before</u> the invasion. So at least some lessons had been learned from the fate of Occupied Europe. That the struggle would have been bloody and drawn out cannot be disputed. But, be that as it may, it remains hypothesis - thanks to the 'Few'.

———— *
    * ————

In the initial stages of the Battle of Britain, the Nazi assault was, for the greater part, strategically directed against the aircraft, airfields, and Chain Home Radar Network of Fighter Command.

The switching of tactics by Goering proved a key factor in the conduct of the War against Germany. His indiscriminate bombing of London demanded retaliation and the bombing of Berlin during the Battle proved more than a gesture of defiance. Goering had boasted that no enemy bomber would fly over the Reich and thus, he irretrievably lost face.

Adolf Hitler reacted by promising the German people that the Luftwaffe would destroy England's cities. And to some grim extent this was achieved. Apart from the devastation of our historic Capital, Portsmouth, Plymouth, Southampton and several other cities felt the weight of the Luftwaffe's night assault. But no city suffered as much as Coventry. With its beautiful cathedral razed to the ground, and its streets almost a wilderness of debris, Coventry gave its name to a term used later in bombing jargon - "Coventrate".

Air Chief Marshal Harris, Bomber Command's revered Chief, stated emphatically at that time, that Germany would "reap the whirlwind", * and the layman watching the 'Few' fight the Luftwaffe's hordes in 1940's brilliant summer, could have had no inkling of the obliterating offensive that would be mounted by Bomber Command a few years later.

* "They have sown the wind and they shall reap the whirlwind." Hosea 8 : 7

The Battle of Britain, no doubt the major battle of World War 11, was "won at home" and rightly the 'Few' are immortalized by their victory. But when the twin-engined Dorniers and Heinkels released their bombs over British cities they kindled in the ensuing flames an awful purpose. One which was to send the mighty four-engined Lancasters, Stirlings and Halifaxes into the very heart of Germany to lay waste the enemy's industrial heart, his principal towns and cities, in a maelstrom of "block-buster" and fire-storm havoc. Thus, the Germans reaped their whirlwind.

The bombing offensive against Germany was a vital contribution to ultimate victory, and as such, comes within the scope of this volume under the heading "Effect". Legions of Fighter Command's unsung bomber brethren made awesome sacrifice carrying out their perilous duty. But only one Squadron of Bomber Command stands out in the public mind - the legendary Dambusters. Therefore, included here is a tribute to 617 Squadron which is also intended as a salute to all the men of Bomber Command.

———— * ————
*

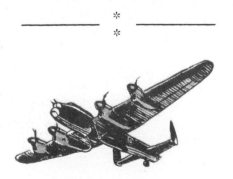

THE DAMBUSTERS

Doctor Barnes Wallis with brilliant plan, gave Six
  One Seven Squadron birth;
Guy Gibson was the chosen man to prove his unique
  weapon's worth.
Air Marshal Cochrane with genius mind, translated
  theories into fact;
A tedious process much-refined by "Chiefy" Powell's
  all-knowing tact.
For weeks they practised flying low, devizing special
  bombing sights
Of wood and nails to distance show - for altitude two
  focussed lights.
The night of May Sixteenth they went - from Scampton
  nineteen Lancasters
Into the German Ruhr were sent - the epoch-making
  Dambusters.
For Gibson, Martin, "Dinghy"-Young; Maudslay,
  Shannon, Maltby, Rice -
Their hero crews with names unsung; one name
  records their sacrifice - "The Dambusters".
Hopgood, Astell, Townsend, Knight; Barlow, Munro,
  Brown and Byers -
All flew on the epic flight, that ever names its dauntless
  fliers - "The Dambusters".
Ottley, Anderson, Burpee too, with "Yank" McCarthy
  on that night,
Lancaster special bombers flew, and forged a legend
  with their flight.

Thro' devastating fiery-flak; to Eder, Moehne, and
  Sorpe they flew.
Relentless in their low attack, the Squadron's losses
  quickly grew.
Guy Gibson made attack at first; his bomb was gone -
  the dam remained.
He then directed each man's burst - and drew the flak
  whilst others aimed - the King of the Dambusters!
The weapon worked!   The dams burst through, then
  thro' the hills they winged for home.
But only ten of them still flew to make it back to
  Scampton 'drome - ten valiant Dambusters.
To all the men who braved the flak; the many killed
  along the way,
And those who lived to make it back - we raise our
  glass to them and say -
        "To the Dambusters!"

TODAY THEIR SHRINE

Seek no dead fire in marble mausoleums!
Nor monuments magnificently high,
Inlaid with mis-spent gold,
To them now worthless.
Such fashionings
Show dedicated crafts in seemly splendour,
While glittered sombre-scripts
Display to curious or patronising eyes
Implied acceptance of a price
Beyond compute,
Electron or of minds.
Our Page of Sacrifice owns no full list
While Patriots perpetuate its lines -
And daily die.

Hear not the kindly utterings of those
Portraying unknown sites
Where long-dead bones
And socket-skulls may lie.
'Tis sentiment and matters not
To age-abandoned flesh and frames,
Their relay run,
The baton ours today.
Be sure they live!
In all the things their sacrifice has bought us;
In history's bloody print;
In times we knew.
But this above all else -
In us!

TODAY THEIR SHRINE

Our day, their shrine
Which taller grows tomorrow.
Tho' founded here
It towers aloof to stars.
Intangible but seen
Thro' memory's glass.
While Resolution holds the lead they won;
While living Courage triumphs o'er Despair;
While their Example bids us Battle on;
Till Death's grim Umpire says our stint is run.
No tribute-gold nor coward's coin
May buy or mortgage that Eternal Cup
Which Love endows and Time engraves
With all their yesterdays and our tomorrows.

THE ROYAL AIR FORCE
BENEVOLENT FUND

(Registered under the War Charities Act 1940 and the Charities Act 1960)

Taken from original German combat photograph—Spitfire going down in flames

*"Never in the field of human conflict was so much owed
by so many to so few"*

(Mr. Winston Churchill, 1940)

PLEASE HELP TO REPAY THE DEBT WE OWE

PATRON: HER MAJESTY THE QUEEN

PRESIDENT: H.R.H. THE DUKE OF KENT, G.C.M.G., G.C.V.O.

CHAIRMAN OF COUNCIL: SIR HARALD PEAKE.

All donations mentioning EIGHTY FOUR DAYS (cheques and postal orders made out to the Royal Air Force Benevolent Fund and crossed "a/c payee") will be personally acknowledged by the Author.

POET AND BEGGAR

I ain't ashamed to beg, Mate, even tho' I'm orften
    shunned,
'Cos I'm beggin' fer our Air Forse an' its Bennyvolunt
    Fund.
Can I twist yore arm, ole Matey, fer a sub of notes or
    pence
To the Airmen of our Country wot 'eld fast in brave
    defence,
Wot Shakespeer corled 'this preshus plot' from 'Itler's
    graspin' paw,
An' knocked 'is ole Looftwaffers down in England by
    the score?
'Cos every quid you 'elp ter raise will do an orful lot
In aidin' blokes in wheelchairs now - which many 'ave
    forgot.
An' sum of 'em 'ave garstly burns, an' sum of 'em
    can't see.
But orl of 'em wound-up that way so's likes of you
    an' me
Can make our forchunes, 'ave our cars, an' do as we
    fink right
(Which wouldn't quite 'ave bin the case if they 'ad lorst
    our fight!)
So if you'll 'elp 'em, Matey, I will write you fanks
    galore -
Wiv addid fanks from my ole mate, the Fund's Air
    Commodore.

IN CONCLUSION

So that is that; my busy pen retiring;
Has lived again that distant Battle's rage;
Within these lines, the Hurricanes, still firing,
Formate with Spitfires on another page.
Called back awhile; those feathered vapour banners
Which fateful winds entangled to ensnare
The flying pawns of tyrant plots and planners
That sprinkled Satan's spawn on summer air.

Remembered in a rhyme; forgotten heroes;
Perhaps a leader or some simple folk;
Deploring those statistic-rounding zeros,
Named those who saved us from the Nazi yolk;
Portrayed alike the tragedy and humour,
Maybe an incident, untold as yet,
Will scotch an old perpetuated rumour
Or bring to mind some long-abandoned bet.

My task complete; my metred Group can scramble,
My stanza Squadrons, flying rhyme to rhyme,
Take-off to face the publisher's preamble;
With couplets roaring they commence the climb.
Although a verse or two may fly unsteady,
I scrawl the manuscript that gives them flight
And thro' the errors I can see already,
Hope some may glimpse that Great Immortal Fight.

168

A CHAPLAIN'S EPILOGUE

There are few signatures of the many on the wall of the Pub in Brasted which do not evoke for me an eager young face. It is a sad comment on our life and times that a war alone calls out that spirit of total self generosity, at least in the scarcely adult, which we look for in vain in peace.

This was surely the first battle in history when young men went out to fight, day after day, straight from their own Kentish countryside and from their wives and sweethearts. For much of the Battle, the squadrons were unable to have quarters in the Mess which was destroyed.

Tommy Lund, Gordon Brettel and Wimpey Wade were often in our house at Westerham, and Wade borrowed the house for his honeymoon. I have a postcard from his German prison from Gordon Brettel, who was one of the sixty officers shot by the Gestapo after the Great Escape. It was sad that Wimpey was killed testing for Hawkers at Dunsfold in 1951 having survived the war.

I see in my log book that I flew 100 hours during my two years at Biggin Hill. The rule was that Chaplains should not fly solo. But no one seemed to notice that when pilots went on leave in the Miles Magister or the Tiger Moth these aeroplanes found their own way back to the dispersal points unaided.

I had the privilege of knowing very many of them better than I might have done in other ways. I remember a Tiger Moth journey with Wade to Bedford at a time when he was not allowed to fly Spitfires because of his persistence in appearing upside down over 92 Squadron Headquarters.

Sometimes it is forgotten that the outcome was most uncertain, and something I wrote at the time about marriage may reflect what many of my friends felt in their hearts while they fought with their heads and their hands.

———————— * ————————
*

1940 MARRIAGE

In thee, in me,
Sweet love, I see
A great and noble company,
A host of men who, dead long past,
Yet in us live and in us last.
Within us two, is there a line
Of those who'll live in coming time
Less torn, perhaps, by war?

Heredity;
Posterity;
For thou art She, and I am He,
Within us past and future meet,
The present mire engulfs our feet;
These muddied gifts our parents gave;
We do not thank.   More grief the grave
Did not engulf them too.

Fertility?
Sterility?
I doubt much which most sad may be.
The worst glooms of antiquity
Cannot have shed so thick a pall
Even when vinegar and gall
He drank there followed Easter light.
This cruel, relentless, lethal night
Destroys our babe unborn.

DECEMBER 1940   DOUGLAS O'HANLON
                 Chaplain (C of E) RAFVR

A complete dictionary of the terms used in the RAF during 1940 would be a sizable volume, but an attempt to clarify and preserve some of the banter used by the 'Few' is offered. Many terms were coined only to be quickly discarded in the light of changing circumstance and technical progress. But those included are largely the significant survivors and the most long-lived. All the terms given are by no means essential to the uninformed reader of this volume. However, a few are used and therefore explained.

———————— * ————————
*

GLOSSARY

An ANGEL meant a thousand feet of altitude, whereby, 'Angels - twelve' would simply mean, 'I'm now
twelve thousand high'.
ARTHUR MITCHELL meant Air Ministry - in short
the stamp 'A.M.' appeared on every single thing
they issued out to them.
BANDITS was the term they used denoting Nazi planes
that sought to paralyse our land and block our
shipping lanes.
BINT meant 'bird', a girl, a dame - a popsy if you like,
girls drove the petrol bowsers and many rode a bike.
BODS were blokes of any sort - in general terms 'a
bod' denoted anyone about - some ordinary - some
odd.

BOFFINS were the brainy types that thought up all the 'mods' - the scientist inventor types - the slide-rule wielding bods.

BOILER was a slang term used for engine - it would seem to couple with that other term of 'pressing on full steam'.

BOUGHT IT meant a chap was killed - whenever it was said it didn't seem to sound as bad as saying he was dead.

BRYLCREEM BOYS - the RAF all gay and debonair, with polished shoes, clean shirt each day - and Brylcreem on their hair.

BURTON same as 'Bought it' - as if he'd joined some queue. 'Gone for a Burton' was a phrase that advertised that brew.

BUSTER meant full engine power with throttles thro' the gate, and engines boosted thus for long might well disintegrate!

CARPET was the same as 'deck' - tho' sounding more serene and probably owed influence to England's pastures green.

CLOBBER meant to knock about with consequences grim - you never knocked a Nazi out - you simply clobbered him.

CLOT meant clown or idiot - a proper clumsy clot, was one who always messed things up - some comical - some not!

DECK alluded to the ground - an aircraft flying low was said to be 'down on the deck' - as far as one dare go.

DITCH described the Channel - the grave of many planes, and 'ditching' meant to flop on it - I hope that this explains.

DRINK meant Channel just the same - the difference I think was no one crashed into the ditch - they went into the drink.

ERKS were all the other ranks - the ground crews and the rest of all the hundred types that kept the air-craft at their best.

FLAMER was a fiery burn of aircraft going down with oily smudge that etched the sky with plume of dirty brown.

HOSING was a term they used describing squirts of lead that splashed in streaming beauty as the tracer bullets sped.

HUNTER meant a fighter plane that sought its airborne goal, collectively their R.T. code would be 'Hunter Patrol'.

KITE - a term for aeroplane, first used in early flight that still survives and yet today some chaps still fly a kite.

MODS meant alterations in ways of doing things, it could refer to tactics or redesigning wings.

NOGGIN was the slang for 'head' - or pints from out the trough, you either knocked a noggin back or knocked his noggin off.

PANCAKE was the order at end of battle's gruel, or uneventful mission, to land, rearm, refuel.

PEEL-OFF from a formation - a very pretty sight - each plane would bank and then slice down to pick a a man to fight.

PRANG meant crash or damage, or someone's praises sang; a term of great endearment was 'Good show! Oh, wizard prang!

R.T. referred to radio - transmitters linking planes with Squadron Leaders in the air or ground controlling brains.

SCRAMBLE in the literal sense of pilots to their kites when every second counted to reach depicted heights.

SNAPPERS were the fighters forming escort for attack, and one flew like the clappers when their cannon sought your back.

SPROG - a brand new pilot or anyone brand new, to rank or some position 'with very little clue'.

SWANNING meant to gad about or going it alone - or chasing after Nazis in planes that were 'test flown'.

TALLY HO! - the sighting call they borrowed from the Hunt - replacing foxes Nazi planes were those that bore the brunt.

TWITCH - a nervous ailment among the flying men whose nerve was stretched beyond all call yet still was stretched again.

VICS divided squadrons in section groups of three, red and yellow, blue and green formated in a vee.

WAFFLE - a gentle crazy flight - a switch-back shallow dive, often said of planes that flew with no one left alive.

WIZARD meaning wonderful - I think they used it 'cos, before the War they made a film of one who lived in Oz.

APPENDICES*

1. THE BATTLE OF BRITAIN - Facsimile of the
   Ministry of Information Booklet issued on behalf
   of the Air Ministry and distributed nationwide in
   1941.
2. Facsimile Anti-Invasion leaflets issued nationwide.

* The material in the Appendices is Crown copyright
and is reproduced by kind permission of the Controller,
Her Majesty's Stationery Office.

AUTHOR'S NOTE

In a dispatch submitted to the Secretary of State
for Air on August 20th 1941, Air Chief Marshal Sir
Hugh C. T. Dowding, A. O. C.-in-C. Fighter Command,
described the Air Ministry's publication THE BATTLE
OF BRITAIN as "an admirable account of the Battle for
public consumption," but pointed out two errors: one,
the overrating of the Hurricane's speed at 335 instead
of 305 mph, of no great importance; the other much
more so: on page 31, it is stated that ".....the fighter
squadrons of the Royal Air Force.....were indeed
stronger at the end of the battle than at the beginning."
In fact, said Dowding, "The majority of the squadrons
had been reduced to the status of training units, and
were fit only for operations against unescorted
bombers."

THE

BATTLE

OF

BRITAIN

AUGUST–OCTOBER 1940